COLLECTED POEMS

TWO DEER: sculpture by Annie Wright. *Photo: Robert P. Thompson*

COLLECTED POEMS

BY

James Wright

56931

WESLEYAN UNIVERSITY PRESS

Middletown, Connecticut

Copyright © 1951, 1956, 1957, 1958, 1959, 1960, 1961, 1962, 1963, 1964, 1965, 1966, 1967, 1968, 1969, 1970, 1971 by James Wright

For permission to reprint some of these poems and for assigning copyrights to him, the author wishes to make due acknowledgment to the editors of the following periodicals and books:

Assay; Atlantic Monthly; Audience; Avon Book of Modern Writing No. 1; Best Articles and Stories; Big Table; Botteghe Oscure; Chelsea; Chicago Review; Choice; The Distinctive Voice; The Fifties; Fresco; The Guinness Book of Poetry; Harper's Bazaar; Harper's Magazine; Hika; Hudson Review; Kenyon Review; London Magazine; Minnesota Review; The Nation; New American Review; New Orleans Poetry Journal; The New Poets of England and America; New World Writing No. 9; The New York Times; Pacific Spectator; Paris Review; Quarterly Review of Literature; Saturday Review; Sense and Sensibility in Twentiety-Century Writing; Sewanee Review; The Sixties; Stand; Truth; University of Connecticut Fine Arts Magazine; University of Kansas City Review; Western Review; Where Is Vietnam?; Yale Review; and Yale University Press, original publisher of his book *The Green Wall.*

Several of these poems first appeared in *The New Yorker,* including "Before a Cashier's Window in a Department Store," "By a Lake in Minnesota," "Echo for the Promise of Georg Trakl's Life," "Evening," "For the Marsh's Birthday," "Poems to a Brown Cricket," "The Quest," "Red Jacket's Grave," "A Secret Gratitude," "Speak," "What the Earth Asked Me," and "My Grandmother's Ghost."

Among poems that first appeared in *Poetry* are "The Life," "The Lights in the Hallway," "Listening to Mourners," "Old Age Compensation," "Outside Fargo, North Dakota," and "Sitting in a Small Screenhouse on a Summer Morning."

The translations from Jiménez first appeared in *Fresco.* Those from Guillén were originally printed in *Cantico: A Selection,* edited by Norman Thomas di Giovanni. Those from Neruda, Trakl, and Vallejo were first published in *Twenty Poems of Pablo Neruda, Twenty Poems of Georg Trakl,* and *Twenty Poems of César Vallejo,* under the editorship of Robert Bly.

Thanks are due to Mr. John Crowe Ransom and his associates for the Kenyon Review Fellowship in Poetry (1958), which made possible the completion of *Saint Judas.* The author is grateful also to three particular friends: Miss Mary Bly, for herself and for the poem which bears her name; Heinrich Heine, for his beautiful song "Aus alten Märchen winkt es"; and Allen Tate, for his friendship in a difficult time.

ISBN : 0–8195–4031–5
Library of Congress Catalog Card Number: 70–142727
Manufactured in the United States of America
First printing April 1971; second printing June 1972

ANNIE

The flowers on the wallpaper spring alive.
                                   Guillén

CONTENTS

SOME TRANSLATIONS

THE BRANCH WILL NOT BREAK

SHALL WE GATHER AT THE RIVER

NEW POEMS

xii

COLLECTED POEMS

THE QUEST

In pasture where the leaf and wood
Were lorn of all delicious apple,
And underfoot a long and supple
Bough leaned down to dip in mud,
I came before the dark to stare
At a gray nest blown in a swirl,
As in the arm of a dead girl
Crippled and torn and laid out bare.

On a hill I came to a bare house,
And crept beside its bleary windows,
But no one lived in those gray hollows,
And rabbits ate the dying grass.
I stood upright, and beat the door,
Alone, indifferent, and aloof
To pebbles rolling down the roof
And dust that filmed the deadened air.

High and behind, where twilight chewed
Severer planes of hills away,
And the bonehouse of a rabbit lay
Dissolving by the darkening road,
I came, and rose to meet the sky,
And reached my fingers to a nest
Of stars laid upward in the west;
They hung too high; my hands fell empty.

So, as you sleep, I seek your bed
And lay my careful, quiet ear
Among the nestings of your hair,
Against your tenuous, fragile head,
And hear the birds beneath your eyes
Stirring for birth, and know the world
Immeasurably alive and good,
Though bare as rifted paradise.

SITTING IN A SMALL SCREENHOUSE
ON A SUMMER MORNING

Ten more miles, it is South Dakota.
Somehow, the roads there turn blue,
When no one walks down them.
One more night of walking, and I could have become
A horse, a blue horse, dancing
Down a road, alone.

I have got this far. It is almost noon. But never mind time:
That is all over.
It is still Minnesota.
Among a few dead cornstalks, the starving shadow
Of a crow leaps to his death.
At least, it is green here,
Although between my body and the elder trees
A savage hornet strains at the wire screen.
He can't get in yet.

It is so still now, I hear the horse
Clear his nostrils.
He has crept out of the green places behind me.
Patient and affectionate, he reads over my shoulder
These words I have written.
He has lived a long time, and he loves to pretend
No one can see him.
Last night I paused at the edge of darkness,
And slept with green dew, alone.
I have come a long way, to surrender my shadow
To the shadow of a horse.

4

from THE GREEN WALL

A FIT AGAINST THE COUNTRY

The stone turns over slowly,
Under the side one sees
The pale flint covered wholly
With whorls and prints of leaf.
After the moss rubs off
It gleams beneath the trees,
Till all the birds lie down.
Hand, you have held that stone.

The sparrow's throat goes hollow,
When the tense air forebodes
Rain to the sagging willow
And leaves the pasture moist.
The slow, cracked song is lost
Far up and down wet roads,
Rain drowns the sparrow's tongue.
Ear, you have heard that song.

Suddenly on the eye
Feathers of morning fall,
Tanagers float away
To sort the blackberry theft.
Though sparrows alone are left
To sound the dawn, and call
Awake the heart's gray dolor,
Eye, you have seen bright color.

Odor of fallen apple
Met you across the air,
The yellow globe lay purple
With bruises underfoot;
And, ravished out of thought,
Both of you had your share,
Sharp nose and watered mouth,
Of the dark tang of earth.

Yet, body, hold your humor
Away from the tempting tree,

The grass, the luring summer
That summon the flesh to fall.
Be glad of the green wall
You climbed across one day,
When winter stung with ice
That vacant paradise.

THE SEASONLESS

When snows begin to fill the park,
It is not hard to keep the eyes
Secure against the flickering dark,
Aware of summer ghosts that rise.
The blistered trellis seems to move
The memory toward root and rose,
The empty fountain fills the air
With spray that spangled women's hair;
And men who walk this park in love
May bide the time of falling snows.

The trees recall their greatness now;
They were not always vague and bowed
With loads that build the slender bough
Till branches bear a tasteless fruit.
A month ago they rose and bore
Fleshes of berry, leaf, and shade:
How painlessly a man recalls
The stain of green on crooked walls,
The summer never known before,
The garden heaped to bloom and fade.

Beyond the holly bush and path
The city lies to meet the night,
And also there the quiet earth
Relies upon the lost delight
To rise again and fill the dark
With waterfalls and swallows' sound.
Beyond the city's lazy fume,
The sea repeats the fall of spume,

And gulls remember cries they made
When lovers fed them off the ground.

But lonely underneath a heap
Of overcoat and crusted ice,
A man goes by, and looks for sleep.
The spring of everlastingness.
Nothing about his face revives
A longing to evade the cold.
The night returns to keep him old,
And why should he, the lost and lulled,
Pray for the night of vanished lives,
The day of girls blown green and gold?

THE HORSE

. . . the glory of his nostrils is terrible.
                    Job 39:20

He kicked the world, and lunging long ago
Rose dripping with the dew of lawns,
Where new wind tapped him to a frieze
Against a wall of rising autumn leaves.
Some young foolhardy dweller of the barrows,
To grip his knees around the flanks,
Leaped from a tree and shivered in the air.
Joy clawed inside the bones
And flesh of the rider at the mane
Flopping and bounding over the dark banks.

Joy and terror floated on either side
Of the rider rearing. The supreme speed
Jerked to a height so spaced and wide
He seemed among the areas of the dead.
The flesh was free, the sky was rockless, clear,
The road beneath the feet was pure, the soul
Spun naked to the air
And lanced against a solitary pole
Of cumulus, to curve and roll

With the heave that disdains
Death in the body, stupor in the brains.

Now we have coddled the gods away.
The cool earth, the soft earth, we say:
Cover our eyes with petals, let the sky
Drift on while we are watching water pass
Among the drowsing mass
Of red and yellow algae in green lanes.
Yet earth contains
The horse as a remembrancer of wild
Arenas we avoid.

One day a stallion whirled my riding wife,
Whose saddle rocked her as a cradled child,
Gentle to the swell of water; yet her life
Poised perilously as on a shattered skiff.
The fear she rode, reminded of the void
That flung the ancient rider to the cold,
Dropped her down. I tossed my reins,

I ran to her with breath to make her rise,
And brought her back. Across my arms
She fumbled for the sunlight with her eyes.
I knew that she would never rest again,
For the colts of the dusk rear back their hooves
And paw us down, the mares of the dawn stampede
Across the cobbled hills till the lights are dead.
Here it is not enough to pray that loves
Draw grass over our childhood's lake of slime.
Run to the rocks where horses cannot climb,
Stable the daemon back to shaken earth,
Warm your hands at the comfortable fire,
Cough in a dish beside a wrinkled bed.

THE FISHERMEN

We tossed our beer cans down among the rocks,
And walked away.

We turned along the beach to wonder
How many girls were out to swim and burn.
We found old men:

The driftwood faces
Sprawled in the air
And patterned hands half hidden in smoke like ferns;
The old men, fishing, letting the sea fall out,
Their twine gone slack.

You spoke of saurian beards
Grown into layers of lime,
Of beetles' shards and broad primeval moths
Lashing great ferns;
Of bent Cro-Magnon mothers beating
Their wheat to mash;
And salty stones
Stuck to the fin and scale
Of salmon skeleton,
And lonely fabulous whorls of wood
Drawn to the shore,
The carping nose, the claws, not to be known
From those dried fishermen:

Who watched the speedboat swaying in the scum
A mile offshore,
Or, nearer, leaping fish
Butting the baby ducks before their climb;
And last of all, before the eyes of age,
The calves of graceful women flashing fast
Into the fluffy towels and out of sight.

You pointed with a stick, and told me
How old men mourning the fall
Forget the splendid sea-top combed as clean as bone,
And the white sails.
You showed me how their faces withered
Even as we looked down
To find where they left off and sea began.

And though the sun swayed in the sea,
They were not moved:
Saurian faces still as layered lime,
The nostrils ferned in smoke behind their pipes,
The eyes resting in whorls like shells on driftwood,
The hands relaxing, letting out the ropes;
And they, whispering together,
The beaten age, the dead, the blood gone dumb.

A GIRL IN A WINDOW

Now she will lean away to fold
The window blind and curtain back,
The yellow arms, the hips of gold,
The supple outline fading black,
Bosom availing nothing now,
And rounded shadow of long thighs.
How can she care for us, allow
The shade to blind imagined eyes?

Behind us, where we sit by trees,
Blundering autos lurch and swerve
On gravel, crawling on their knees
Around the unfamiliar curve;
Farther behind, a passing train
Ignores our lost identity;
So, reassured, we turn again
To see her vanish under sky.

Soon we must leave her scene to night,
To stars, or the indiscriminate
Pale accidents of lantern light,
A watchman walking by too late.
Let us return her now, my friends,
Her love, her body to the grave
Fancy of dreams where love depends.
She gave, and did not know she gave.

ON THE SKELETON OF A HOUND

Nightfall, that saw the morning-glories float
Tendril and string against the crumbling wall,
Nurses him now, his skeleton for grief,
His locks for comfort curled among the leaf.
Shuttles of moonlight weave his shadow tall,
Milkweed and dew flow upward to his throat.
Now catbird feathers plume the apple mound,
And starlings drowse to winter up the ground.
Thickened away from speech by fear, I move
Around the body. Over his forepaws, steep
Declivities darken down the moonlight now,
And the long throat that bayed a year ago
Declines from summer. Flies would love to leap
Between his eyes and hum away the space
Between the ears, the hollow where a hare
Could hide; another jealous dog would tumble
The bones apart, angry, the shining crumble
Of a great body gleaming in the air;
Quivering pigeons foul his broken face.
I can imagine men who search the earth
For handy resurrections, overturn
The body of a beetle in its grave;
Whispering men digging for gods might delve
A pocket for these bones, then slowly burn
Twigs in the leaves, pray for another birth.
But I will turn my face away from this
Ruin of summer, collapse of fur and bone.
For once a white hare huddled up the grass,
The sparrows flocked away to see the race.
I stood on darkness, clinging to a stone,
I saw the two leaping alive on ice,
On earth, on leaf, humus and withered vine:
The rabbit splendid in a shroud of shade,
The dog carved on the sunlight, on the air,
Fierce and magnificent his rippled hair,
The cockleburs shaking around his head.
Then, suddenly, the hare leaped beyond pain
Out of the open meadow, and the hound

Followed the voiceless dancer to the moon,
To dark, to death, to other meadows where
Singing young women dance around a fire,
Where love reveres the living.

                    I alone
Scatter this hulk about the dampened ground;
And while the moon rises beyond me, throw
The ribs and spine out of their perfect shape.
For a last charm to the dead, I lift the skull
And toss it over the maples like a ball.
Strewn to the woods, now may that spirit sleep
That flamed over the ground a year ago.
I know the mole will heave a shinbone over,
The earthworm snuggle for a nap on paws,
The honest bees build honey in the head;
The earth knows how to handle the great dead
Who lived the body out, and broke its laws,
Knocked down a fence, tore up a field of clover.

THREE STEPS TO THE GRAVEYARD

When I went there first,
In the spring, it was evening,
It was long hollow thorn
Laid under the locust,
And near to my feet
The crowfoot, the mayapple
Trod their limbs down
Till the stalk blew over.
It grew summer, O riches
Of girls on the lawn,
And boys' locks lying
Tousled on knees,
The picknickers leaving,
The day gone down.

When I went there again,
I walked with my father

14

Who held in his hand
The crowfoot, the mayapple,
And under my hands,
To hold off the sunlight,
I saw him going,
Between two trees;
When the lawn lay empty
It was the year's end,
It was the darkness,
It was long hollow thorn
To wound the bare shade,
The sheaf and the blade.

O now as I go there
The crowfoot, the mayapple
Blear the gray pond;
Beside the still waters
The field mouse tiptoes,
To hear the air sounding
The long hollow thorn.
I lean to the hollow,
But nothing blows there,
The day goes down.
The field mice flutter
Like grass and are gone,
And a skinny old woman
Scrubs at a stone,
Between two trees.

FATHER

In paradise I poised my foot above the boat and said:
Who prayed for me?
                         But only the dip of an oar
In water sounded; slowly fog from some cold shore
Circled in wreaths around my head.

But who is waiting?

And the wind began,
Transfiguring my face from nothingness
To tiny weeping eyes. And when my voice
Grew real, there was a place
Far, far below on earth. There was a tiny man —

It was my father wandering round the waters at the wharf.
Irritably he circled and he called
Out to the marine currents up and down,
But heard only a cold unmeaning cough,
And saw the oarsman in the mist enshawled.

He drew me from the boat. I was asleep.
And we went home together.

ELEGY IN A FIRELIT ROOM

The window showed a willow in the west,
But windy dry. No folly weeping there.
A sparrow hung a wire about its breast
And spun across the air.

Instead of paying winter any mind,
I ran my fingerprints across the glass,
To feel the crystal forest sown by wind,
And one small face:

A child among the frozen bushes lost,
Breaking the white and rigid twigs between
Fingers more heavenly than hands of dust,
And fingernails more clean.

Beyond, the willow would not cry for cold,
The sparrow hovered long enough to stare;
The face between me and the wintered world
Began to disappear;

Because some friendly hands behind my back
Fumbled the coal and tended up the fire.

16

Warmth of the room waved to the window sash,
The face among the forest fell to air.

The glass began to weep instead of eyes,
A slow gray feather floated down the sky.
Delicate bone, finger and bush, and eyes
Yearned to the kissing fire and fell away.

Over the naked pasture and beyond,
A frozen bird lay down among the dead
Weeds, and the willow strode upon the wind
And would not bow its head.

ARRANGEMENTS WITH EARTH
FOR THREE DEAD FRIENDS

Sweet earth, he ran and changed his shoes to go
Outside with other children through the fields.
He panted up the hills and swung from trees
Wild as a beast but for the human laughter
That tumbled like a cider down his cheeks.
Sweet earth, the summer has been gone for weeks,
And weary fish already sleeping under water
Below the banks where early acorns freeze.
Receive his flesh and keep it cured of colds.
Button his coat and scarf his throat from snow.

And now, bright earth, this other is out of place
In what, awake, we speak about as tombs.
He sang in houses when the birds were still
And friends of his were huddled round till dawn
After the many nights to hear him sing.
Bright earth, his friends remember how he sang
Voices of night away when wind was one.
Lonely the neighborhood beneath your hill
Where he is waved away through silent rooms.
Listen for music, earth, and human ways.

Dark earth, there is another gone away,
But she was not inclined to beg of you
Relief from water falling or the storm.
She was aware of scavengers in holes
Of stone, she knew the loosened stones that fell
Indifferently as pebbles plunging down a well
And broke for the sake of nothing human souls.
Earth, hide your face from her where dark is warm.
She does not beg for anything, who knew
The change of tone, the human hope gone gray.

LAMENT FOR MY BROTHER ON A HAYRAKE

Cool with the touch of autumn, waters break
Out of the pump at dawn to clear my eyes;
I leave the house, to face the sacrifice
Of hay, the drag and death. By day, by moon,
I have seen my younger brother wipe his face
And heave his arm on steel. He need not pass
Under the blade to waste his life and break;

The hunching of the body is enough
To violate his bones. That bright machine
Strips the revolving earth of more than grass;
Powered by the fire of summer, bundles fall
Folded to die beside a burlap shroud;
And so my broken brother may lie mown
Out of the wasted fallows, winds return,
Corn-yellow tassels of his hair blow down,
The summer bear him sideways in a bale
Of darkness to October's mow of cloud.

SHE HID IN THE TREES FROM THE NURSES

She stands between the trees and holds
One hand in the other, still.
Now far away the evening folds
Around the siloes and the hill.

18

She sees, slowly, the gardener
Return to check the gate before
The smoke begins to soften the air
And June bugs try the open door.

And through the windows, washing hands,
The patients have the mattress made,
Their trousers felt for colored stones,
The pleasures of the noon recalled:

For some were caught and held for hours
By spiders skating over a pond,
Some parted veils of hollyhocks
And looked for rabbit holes beyond.

But now the trousers lie in rows,
She sees the undressed shadows creep
Through half-illuminated minds
And chase the hare and flower to sleep.

She too must answer summons now,
And play the chimes inside her brain
When whistles of attendants blow;
Yet, for a while, she would remain,

And dabble her feet in the damp grass,
And lean against a yielding stalk,
And spread her name in dew across
The pebbles where the droplets walk.

Minutes away a nurse will come
Across the lawn and call for her;
The starlight calls the robin home,
The swans retire beneath their wings.

Surely her mind is clear enough
To hear her name among the trees.
She must remember home and love
And skirts that sway below her knees.

But why must she desert the shade
And sleep between the walls all night?
Why must a lonely girl run mad
To gain the simple, pure delight

Of staying, when the others leave,
To write a name or hold a stone?
Of hearing bobwhites flute their love
Though buildings loudly tumble down?

TO A DEFEATED SAVIOR

Do you forget the shifting hole
Where the slow swimmer fell aground
And floundered for your fishing pole
Above the snarl of string and sound?
You never seem to turn your face
Directly toward the river side,
Or up the bridge, or anyplace
Near where the skinny swimmer died.

You stand all day and look at girls,
Or climb a tree, or change a tire;
But I have seen the colored swirls
Of water flow to livid fire
Across your sleeping nose and jaws,
Transfiguring both the bone and skin
To muddy banks and sliding shoals
You and the drowned kid tumble in.

You see his face, upturning, float
And bob across your wavering bed;
His wailing fingers call your boat,
His voice throws up the ruddy silt,
The bleary vision prays for light
In sky behind your frozen hands;
But sinking in the dark all night,
You charm the shore with bloomless wands.

The circling tow, the shadowy pool
Shift underneath us everywhere.
You would have raised him, flesh and soul,
Had you been strong enough to dare;
You would have lifted him to breathe,
Believing your good hands would keep
His body clear of your own death:
This dream, this drowning in your sleep.

TO A TROUBLED FRIEND

Weep, and weep long, but do not weep for me,
Nor, long lamenting, raise, for any word
Of mine that beats above you like a bird,
Your voice, or hand. But shaken clear, and free,
Be the bare maple, bough where nests are made
Snug in the season's wrinkled cloth of frost;
Be leaf, by hardwood knots, by tendrils crossed
On tendrils, stripped, uncaring; give no shade.

Give winter nothing; hold; and let the flake
Poise or dissolve along your upheld arms.
All flawless hexagons may melt and break;
While you must feel the summer's rage of fire,
Beyond this frigid season's empty storms,
Banished to bloom, and bear the birds' desire.

POEM FOR KATHLEEN FERRIER

I
I leaned to hear your song,
The breathing and the echo;
And when it dropped away,
I thought, for one deaf moment,
That I could never listen
To any other voice.

2

But the land is deep in sound.
The sleepy hares and crickets
Remember how to cry.
The birds have not forgotten
(The tanager, the sparrow)
The tumbled, rising tone.

3

The sounds go on, and on,
In spite of what the morning
Or evening dark has done.
We have no holy voices
Like yours to lift above us,
Yet we cannot be still.

4

All earth is loud enough.
Then why should I be sorry
(The owl scritches alive)
To stand before a shadow,
And see a cold piano
Half hidden by a drape?

5

No reason I can give.
Uttering tongues are busy,
Mount the diminished air
(The breathing and the echo)
Enough to keep the ear
Half satisfied forever.

A SONG FOR THE MIDDLE OF THE NIGHT

By way of explaining to my son the following curse by
Eustace Deschamps: "Happy is he who has no children;
for babies bring nothing but crying and stench."

Now first of all he means the night
    You beat the crib and cried

And brought me spinning out of bed
    To powder your backside.
I rolled your buttocks over
    And I could not complain:
Legs up, la la, legs down, la la,
    Back to sleep again.

Now second of all he means the day
    You dabbled out of doors
And dragged a dead cat Billy-be-damned
    Across the kitchen floors.
I rolled your buttocks over
    And made you sing for pain:
Legs up, la la, legs down, la la,
    Back to sleep again.

But third of all my father once
    Laid me across his knee
And solved the trouble when he beat
    The yowling out of me.
He rocked me on his shoulder
    When razor straps were vain:
Legs up, la la, legs down, la la,
    Back to sleep again.

So roll upon your belly, boy,
    And bother being cursed.
You turn the household upside down,
    But you are not the first.
Deschamps the poet blubbered too,
    For all his fool disdain:
Legs up, la la, legs down, la la,
    Back to sleep again.

A PRESENTATION OF TWO BIRDS TO MY SON

Chicken. How shall I tell you what it is,
And why it does not float with tanagers?
Its ecstasy is dead, it does not care.

Its children huddle underneath its wings,
And altogether lounge against the shack,
Warm in the slick tarpaulin, smug and soft.

You must not fumble in your mind
The genuine ecstasy of climbing birds
With that dull fowl.
When your grandfather held it by the feet
And laid the skinny neck across
The ragged chopping block,
The flop of wings, the jerk of the red comb
Were a dumb agony,
Stupid and meaningless. It was no joy
To leave the body beaten underfoot;
Life was a flick of corn, a steady roost.
Chicken. The sound is plain.

Look up and see the swift above the trees.
How shall I tell you why he always veers
And banks around the shaken sleeve of air,
Away from ground? He hardly flies on brains;
Pockets of air impale his hollow bones.
He leans against the rainfall or the sun.

You must not mix this pair of birds
Together in your mind before you know
That both are clods.
What makes the chimney swift approach the sky
Is ecstasy, a kind of fire
That beats the bones apart
And lets the fragile feathers close with air.
Flight too is agony,
Stupid and meaningless. Why should it be joy
To leave the body beaten underfoot,
To mold the limbs against the wind, and join
Those clean dark glides of Dionysian birds?
The flight is deeper than your father, boy.

TO A HOSTESS SAYING GOOD NIGHT

Shake out the ruffle, turn and go,
Over the trellis blow the kiss.
Some of the guests will never know
Another night to shadow this.
Some of the birds awake in vines
Will never see another face
So frail, so lovely anyplace
Between the birdbath and the bines.

O dark come never down to you.
I look away and look away:
Over the moon the shadows go,
Over your shoulder, nebulae.
Some of the vast, the vacant stars
Will never see your face at all,
Your frail, your lovely eyelids fall
Between Andromeda and Mars.

A POEM ABOUT GEORGE DOTY
IN THE DEATH HOUSE

Lured by the wall, and drawn
To stare below the roof,
Where pigeons nest aloof
From prowling cats and men,
I count the sash and bar
Secured to granite stone,
And note the daylight gone,
Supper and silence near.

Close to the wall inside,
Immured, empty of love,
A man I have wondered of
Lies patient, vacant-eyed.
A month and a day ago
He stopped his car and found

A girl on the darkening ground,
And killed her in the snow.

Beside his cell, I am told,
Hardy perennial bums
Complain till twilight comes
For hunger and for cold.
They hardly know of a day
That saw their hunger pass.
Bred to the dark, their flesh
Peacefully withers away.

The man who sits alone,
He is the one for wonder,
Who sways his fingers under
The cleanly shaven chin,
Who sees, in the shaving mirror
Pinned to the barren wall,
The uprooted ghost of all:
The simple, easy terror.

Caught between sky and earth,
Poor stupid animal,
Stripped naked to the wall,
He saw the blundered birth
Of daemons beyond sound.
Sick of the dark, he rose
For love, and now he goes
Back to the broken ground.

Now, as he grips the chain
And holds the wall, to bear
What no man ever bore,
He hears the bums complain;
But I mourn no soul but his,
Not even the bums who die,
Nor the homely girl whose cry
Crumbled his pleading kiss.

TO A FUGITIVE

The night you got away, I dreamed you rose
Out of the earth to lean on a young tree.
Then they were there, hulking the moon away,
The great dogs rooting, snuffing up the grass.
You raise a hand, hungry to hold your lips
Out of the wailing air; but lights begin
Spidering the ground; oh they come closing in,
The beam searches your face like fingertips.

Hurry, Maguire, hammer the body down,
Crouch to the wall again, shackle the cold
Machine guns and the sheriff and the cars:
Divide the bright bars of the cornered bone,
Strip, run for it, break the last law, unfold,
Dart down the alley, race between the stars.

ELEUTHERIA

Rubbing her mouth along my mouth she lost
Illusions of the sky, the dreams it offered:
The pale cloud walking home to winter, dust
Blown to a shell of sails so far above
That autumn landscape where we lay and suffered
The fruits of summer in the fields of love.

We lay and heard the apples fall for hours,
The stripping twilight plundered trees of boughs,
The land dissolved beneath the rabbit's heels,
And far away I heard a window close,
A haying wagon heave and catch its wheels,
Some water slide and stumble and be still.
The dark began to climb the empty hill.

If dark Eleutheria turned and lay
Forever beside me, who would care for years?
The throat, the supple belly, the warm thigh

Burgeoned against the earth; I lay afraid,
For who could bear such beauty under the sky?
I would have held her loveliness in air,
Away from things that lured me to decay:
The ground's deliberate riches, fallen pears,
Bewildered apples blown to mounds of shade.

Lovers' location is the first to fade.
They wander back in winter, but there is
No comfortable grass to couch a dress.
Musicians of the yellow weeds are dead.
And she, remembering something, turns to hear
Either a milkweed float or a thistle fall.
Bodiless shadow thrown along a wall,
She glides lightly; the pale year follows her.

The moments ride away, the locust flute
Is silvered thin and lost, over and over.
She will return some evening to discover
The tree uplifted to the very root,
The leaves shouldered away, with lichen grown
Among the interlacings of the stone,
October blowing dust, and summer gone
Into a dark barn, like a hiding lover.

AUTUMNAL

Soft, where the shadow glides,
The yellow pears fell down.
The long bough slowly rides
The air of my delight.

Air, though but nothing, air
Falls heavy down your shoulder.
You hold in burdened hair
The color of my delight.

Neither the hollow pear,
Nor leaf among the grass,

Nor wind that wails the year
Against your leaning ear,
Will alter my delight:

That holds the pear upright
And sings along the bough,
Warms to the mellow sun.
The song of my delight
Gathers about you now,
Is whispered through, and gone.

THE SHADOW AND THE REAL

There was no more than shadow where
She leaned outside the kitchen door,
Stood in the sun and let her hair
Loosely float in the air and fall.
She tossed her body's form before
Her feet, and laid it down the wall.
And how was I to feel, therefore,
Shadow no more than darker air?

I rose, and crossed the room, to find
Her hands, her body, her green dress;
But where she stood, the sun behind
Demolished her from touch and sight.
Her body burned to emptiness,
Her hair caught summer in the light;
I sought, bewildered, for her face,
No more than splendid air, gone blind.

WITCHES WAKEN THE NATURAL WORLD IN SPRING

Warm in the underbough of dark
Willows is where the women go
To whisper how the barren park
Will shiver into blossom now.
It does not matter they are slim

Or plump as melons left too long
Upon the vine; beneath the dim
Spell of the willow they are strong.

And very seldom I remember
What revelations they have spoken.
I know I saw a willow tremble
In starlight once, a burdock broken,
Shaken by the voice of my girl
Who waved to heaven overhead;
And though she made a leaflet fall
I have forgotten what she said:

Except that spring was coming on
Or might have come already while
We lay beside a smooth-veined stone;
Except an owl sang half a mile
Away; except a starling's feather
Softened my face beside a root:
But how should I remember whether
She was the one who spoke, or not?

MORNING HYMN TO A DARK GIRL

Summoned to desolation by the dawn,
I climb the bridge over the water, see
The Negro mount the driver's cabin and wave
Goodbye to the glum cop across the canal,
Goodbye to the flat face amd empty eyes
Made human one more time. That uniform
Shivers and dulls against the pier, is stone.

Now in the upper world, the buses drift
Over the bridge, the gulls collect and fly,
Blown by the rush of rose; aseptic girls
Powder their lank deliberate faces, mount
The fog under the billboards. Over the lake
The windows of the rich waken and yawn.
Light blows across the city, dune on dune.

Caught by the scruff of the neck, and thrown out here
To the pale town, to the stone, to burial,
I celebrate you, Betty, flank and breast
Rich to the yellow silk of bed and floors;
Now half awake, your body blossoming trees;
One arm beneath your neck, you legs uprisen,
You blow dark thighs back, back into the dark.

Your shivering ankles skate the scented air;
Betty, burgeoning your golden skin, you poise
Tracing gazelles and tigers on your breasts,
Deep in the jungle of your bed you drowse;
Fine muscles of the rippling panthers move
And snuggle at your calves; under your arms
Mangoes and melons yearn; and glittering slowly,
Quick parakeets trill in your heavy trees,
O everywhere, Betty, between your boughs.

Pity the rising dead who fear the dark.
Soft Betty, locked from snickers in a dark
Brothel, dream on; scatter the yellow corn
Into the wilderness, and sleep all day.
For the leopards leap into the open grass,
Bananas, lemons fling air, fling odor, fall.
And, gracing darkly the dark light, you flow
Out of the grove to laugh at dreamy boys,
You greet the river with a song so low
No lover on a boat can hear, you slide
Silkily to the water, where you rinse
Your fluted body, fearless; though alive
Orangutans sway from the leaves and gaze,
Crocodiles doze along the oozy shore.

THE QUAIL

Lost in the brush, bound by the other path
To find the house,
You let me know how many voices,
How many shifting bodies you possessed,

How you could flit away to follow birds,
And yet be near.

A quail implored the hollow for a home,
A covey of dark to lie in under stars;
And, when it sang, you left my hand
To voyage how softly down the even grass
And see the meadow where the quails lie down,
Flushed in the dark by hunters' broken guns.

You left my side before I knew the way
To find the house,
And soon you called across the hollow
To say you were alive and still on earth;
And, when you sang, the quail began to cry,
So I lost both.

The blue dusk bore feathers beyond our eyes,
Dissolved all wings as you, your hair dissolved,
Your frame of bone blown hollow as a house
Beside the path, were borne away from me
Farther than birds for whom I did not care,
Comingled with the dark complaining air.

I could have called the simple dark to fade,
To find the house,
And left you standing silent;
But stained away by maple leaves, and led
From tree to tree by wands of luring ghosts,
You knew my love,

You knew my feet would never turn away
From any forest where your body was,
Though vanished up the disembodied dark.
And when I found you laughing under trees,
The quail began to trill and flute away,
As far away as hands that reach for hands;
But, when it sang, you kissed me out of sound.

SAPPHO

Ach, in den Armen hab ich sie alle verloren, du nur, du wirst immer wieder geboren. . . .   RILKE, *Die Aufzeichnungen des Malte Laurids Brigge*

The twilight falls; I soften the dusting feathers,
And clean again.
The house has lain and moldered for three days,
The windows smeared with rain, the curtains torn,
The mice come in,
The kitchen blown with cold.

I keep the house, and say no words.

It is true I am as twisted as the cactus
That gnarls and turns beside the milky light,
That cuts the fingers easily and means nothing,
For all the pain that shoots along the hand.
I dust the feathers down the yellow thorns,
I light the stove.

The gas curls round the iron fretwork, the flame
Floats above the lace,
And bounces like a dancer stayed on air.
Fire does not rest on iron, it drifts like a blue blossom
And catches on my breath;
Coiling, spinning, the blue foam of the gas fire
Writhes like a naked girl;
Turns up its face, like her.

She came to me in rain.
I did not know her, I did not know my name
After she left to bed her children down,
To phone her husband they were gone asleep,
And she, lying, a pure fire, in the feathers,
Dancing above the ironwork of her bed,
Roaring, and singeing nothing.
She had not wound her arms about me then,
She had not dared.
I only took her coat, and smiled to hear

How she had left her purse and her umbrella
In the theater, how she was sopping cold
With the fall rain; and mine was the one light
In the neighborhood. She came to my gas fire
And lay before it, sprawled, her pure bare shoulders
Folded in a doze, a clear, cold curve of stone.

I only leaned above the hair,
Turned back the quilt, arranged the feet, the arms,
And kissed the sleeping shoulder, lightly, like the rain;
And when she woke to wear her weathered clothes,
I sent her home.
She floated, a blue blossom, over the street.

And when she came again,
It was not long before she turned to me,
And let her shawl slide down her neck and shoulder,
Let her hair fall.
And when she came again,
It did not rain.

Her husband came to pluck her like an apple,
As the drunken farmer lurches against the tree,
Grips the green globe not long beyond its bloom,
And tears the skin, brutally, out of the bark,
Leaves the whole bough broken,
The orchard torn with many footprints,
The fence swung wide
On a raw hinge.

And now it is said of me
That my love is nothing because I have borne no children,
Or because I have fathered none;
That I twisted the twig in my hands
And cut the blossom free too soon from the seed;
That I lay across the fire,
And snuffed it dead sooner than draft or rain.

But I have turned away, and drawn myself
Upright to walk along the room alone.

Across the dark the spines of cactus plants
Remind me how I go — aloof, obscure,
Indifferent to the words the children chalk
Against my house and down the garden walls.
They cannot tear the garden out of me,
Nor smear my love with names. Love is a cliff,
A clear, cold curve of stone, mottled by stars,
Smirched by the morning, carved by the dark sea
Till stars and dawn and waves can slash no more,
Till the rock's heart is found and shaped again.

I keep the house and say no words, the evening
Falls like a petal down the shawl of trees.
I light the fire and see the blossom dance
On air alone; I will not douse that flame,
That searing flower; I will burn in it.
I will not banish love to empty rain.

For I know that I am asked to hate myself
For their sweet sake
Who sow the world with child.
I am given to burn on the dark fire they make
With their sly voices.

But I have burned already down to bone.
There is a fire that burns beyond the names
Of sludge and filth of which this world is made.
Agony sears the dark flesh of the body,
And lifts me higher than the smoke, to rise
Above the earth, above the sacrifice;
Until my soul flares outward like a blue
Blossom of gas fire dancing in mid-air:
Free of the body's work of twisted iron.

A GESTURE BY A LADY WITH AN ASSUMED NAME

Letters she left to clutter up the desk
Burned in the general gutter when the maid

Came in to do the room and take the risk
Of slipping off the necklace round her head.

Laundry she left to clutter up the floor
Hung to rachitic skeletons of girls
Who worked the bars or labored up the stair
To crown her blowsy ribbons on their curls.

Lovers she left to clutter up the town
Mourned in the chilly morgue and went away,
All but the husbands sneaking up and down
The stairs of that apartment house all day.

What were they looking for? The cold pretense
Of lamentation offered in a stew?
A note? A gift? A shred of evidence
To love when there was nothing else to do?

Or did they rise to weep for that unheard–
Of love, whose misery cries and does not care
Whether or not the madam hears a word
Or skinny children watch the trodden stair?

Whether or not, how could she love so many,
Then turn away to die as though for none?
I saw the last offer a child a penny
To creep outside and see the cops were gone.

MUTTERINGS OVER THE CRIB OF A DEAF CHILD

"How will he hear the bell at school
Arrange the broken afternoon,
And know to run across the cool
Grasses where the starlings cry,
Or understand the day is gone?"

Well, someone lifting curious brows
Will take the measure of the clock.
And he will see the birchen boughs

Outside sagging dark from the sky,
And the shade crawling upon the rock.

"And how will he know to rise at morning?
His mother has other sons to waken,
She has the stove she must build to burning
Before the coals of the nighttime die;
And he never stirs when he is shaken."

I take it the air affects the skin,
And you remember, when you were young,
Sometimes you could feel the dawn begin,
And the fire would call you, by and by,
Out of the bed and bring you along.

"Well, good enough. To serve his needs
All kinds of arrangements can be made.
But what will you do if his finger bleeds?
Or a bobwhite whistles invisibly
And flutes like an angel off in the shade?"

He will learn pain. And, as for the bird,
It is always darkening when that comes out.
I will putter as though I had not heard,
And lift him into my arms and sing
Whether he hears my song or not.

THE ANGEL

Last night, before I came to bear
The clean edge of my wing upon the boulder,
I walked about the town.
The people seemed at peace that he was dead:
A beggar carried water out of a door,
And young men gathered round the corner
To spell the night.

I walked, like a folded bird, about the towers
And sang softly to the blue levels of evening,

I slid down treeless, featherless, bemused:
At curious faces whispering round a fire
And sniffing chestnuts sugared by a woman;
At a vague child heaving a beetle over
In dust, to see it swimming on its back.

Under an arch I found a woman lean
Weeping for loneliness: away from her
A young man whistle toward the crowds;
Out of an open window pigeons flew
And a slow dove fluted for nothing — the girl
Blew to the air a melody lost on me.

Laid in a pile of stone, how could he weep
For that calm town?
Looped in a yoke of darkened garden,
He murmured blood out of his heart for love,
Hallowed a soldier, took the savage kiss
And gave it back a warm caress;

Yet no one changed.

Tossing aside the worry of the place,
As someone threw an apple core across
A wall I walked beside, I sought delight
Pebble by pebble, song by song, and light
By light, singly, among the river boats.
Down to the river at the end I came.

But then a girl appeared, to wash her hair.
Struck stupid by her face,
I stood there, sick to love her, sick of sky.
The child, the beetle, chestnut fires, the song
Of girl and dove
Shuddered along my wings and arms.
She slipped her bodice off, and a last wave
Of shadow oiled her shoulder till it shone;
Lifting her arms to loosen the soft braids
She looked across the water. I looked down
And felt my wings waving aside the air,

Furious to fly. For I could never bear
Belly and breast and thigh against the ground.

Now, having heaved the hidden hollow open
As I was sent to do, seen Jesus waken
And guided the women there, I wait to rise.
To feel a weapon gouge between the ribs,
He hung with a shut mouth:
For curious faces round a chestnut fire,
For the slow fluting doves
Lost on a trellis, for the laughing girl
Who frightened me away.

But now I fumble at the single joy
Of dawn. On the pale ruffle of the lake
The ripples weave a color I can bear.
Under a hill I see the city sleep
And fade. The perfect pleasure of the eyes:
A tiny bird bathed in a bowl of air,
Carving a yellow ripple down the bines,
Posing no storm to blow my wings aside
As I drift upward dropping a white feather.

THE ASSIGNATION

After the winter thawed away, I rose,
Remembering what you said. Below the field
Where I was dead, the crinkled leaf and blade
Summoned my body, told me I must go.
Across the road I saw some other dead
Revive their little fires, and bow the head
To someone still alive and long ago.
Low in the haze a pall of smoke arose.

Inside the moon's hollow is a hale gray man
Who washed his hands, and waved me where to go:
Up the long hill, the mound of lunar snow,
Around three lapping pebbles, over the crossed
Arms of an owl nailed to the southern sky.

I spun three times about, I scattered high,
Over my shoulder, clouds of salt and dust.
The earth began to clear. I saw a man.

He said the sun was falling toward the trees,
The picnic nearly over. Small on the lake
The sails were luring lightning out of dark,
While quieter people guided slim canoes.
I hid in bushes, shy. Already cars
Shuttled away, the earliest evening stars
Blurred in a cloud. A lone child left his shoes
Half in the sand, and slept beneath the trees.

With fires demolished, everybody gone
To root in bushes, congregate by trees
Or haul the yellow windows down to haze,
I lost my way. Water in water fell,
The badgers nibbled rootlets up the shore,
For dancing more than food, where long before
Women had gossiped. Chanting a soft farewell,
Canaries swung. Then everything was gone.

No hurry for me there, I let my dress
Fall to the lawn, the pleasure of the silk
Wind with the subtle grass, berries and milk
Of skin sweeten me. Snuggling, I lay prone,
Barren yet motherly for what might come

Out of the emptied branches, man or flame.
I shivered slightly. Everything was gone,
Everyone gone. I kicked aside my dress.

O then it was you I waited for, to hold
The soft leaves of my bones between your hands
And warm them back to life, to fashion wands
Out of my shining arms. O it was you
I loved before my dying and long after,
You, you I could not find. The air fell softer,
My snatch of breath gave out, but no one blew
My name in hallowed weeds. Lonely to hold

40

Some hand upon me, lest it float away
And be as dead as I, thrown in a sack
Of air to drown in air, I rose, lay back
In trees, and died again. The spiders care
For trellises they hold against the sky,
Except for walls of air the houses die
And fall; and only for my flesh of air
Your flesh of earth would lean and drift away;

But you cared nothing, living, false to me.
What could I do but take a daemon then
And slouch about in dust, eager for pain
Or anything, to keep your memory clear?
A thing came down from the dark air on wings
And rummaged at my limbs, to hold my wings
Down in the dirt; I could not see for fear.
The thing withdrew, full of the dark and me.

And I was riven. Even my poor ghost
Can never stand beside your window now;
I stir the wind, I chatter at a bough,
But make no sound. Your cowardice may keep
You from your assignation with my ghost,
The love you promised me when I was dust,
Not air. And yet I cannot even sleep,
I cannot die, but I will feel my ghost

Driven to find this orchard every year,
This picnic ground, and wait till everyone
Tires of the sundown, turns the headlights on,
To float them off like moths into the dark.
I will stand up to strip my hunger off,
And stare, and mumble, knowing all your love
Is cut beside my name on the white rock,
While you forget the promise and the year.

You sat beside the bed, you took my hands;
And when I lay beyond all speech, you said,
You swore to love me after I was dead,
To meet me in a grove and love me still,

Love the white air, the shadow where it lay.
Dear love, I called your name in air today,
I saw the picnic vanish down the hill,
And waved the moon awake, with empty hands.

COME FORTH

Lazarus lay to see the body turn.
The femur first removed itself from arms,
The elbows folded under each other soon.

The clavicle and vertebrae and shin
Divided like the stars and let the air
Caress the flesh awake before it fell.

Only the torpid brain would not remove.
From far away beyond the granite walls
A vowel of longing tore the wind in two.

Come forth, it said. *But who is this who cried?*
For I have left the human long ago,
My flesh a synagogue the flame has eaten.

Before the voice the worms began to pray,
And fled away howling into the granite.
The shin returned to spring a leaping leg,

The skull rounded itself upon the brain,
The heart arose and cried with joy for pain,
The arteries assumed a thud again.

And the hair furied on the shocking head,
And muscles blossomed like the thunderhead
That trumpets the pale tropics to green storm.

The stones rolling away and the air thrust
Into the lung of the cave, Lazarus knew
The unholy and indifferent sting of wind

42

Across the flesh of man. Outside, the sun
Flayed the same bone as before. Nevertheless
His treading skeleton clattered like a choir

And waved him forward on a crest of praise.
A wall or two away the calling voice
Shook like a pacing father, and was still.

O blessed fire, O harsh and loving air.

ERINNA TO SAPPHO

I saw your shoulder swell and pitch
Alive, your fingers, curving, turn
To summon me above that ditch
    Where I lay down.

Yet as I came, you turned about
And waved to someone out of sight,
Someone you could not do without
    That very night.

Who was she? for I only saw
Mellifluous berries fall from vines,
Long apple blooms depress a bough,
    Clustering wines

Dripping their liquor as they hung
In spray and tendril, curling hair.
You flickered your inviting tongue
    At no one there;

No one but air, garden, the hewn
Poet above his pedestal,
Lyre in the marble, song in stone,
    The trees, the wall;

Unless there was, before I rose,
One of the hollow things who walk

The world in anguish, wearing clothes
    Just before dark;

And you were calling out to her
Or him, whatever bodiless
Presences hollow spirits bear
    Beneath their dress.

Whether I knew or did not know,
Under the misery of my skin,
What pale plunderer looted you
    Outside and in,

I leaped, above the ditch of earth,
Bodily, clung my arms around
Your poising knees, and brought us both
    Back to the ground,

Where we belong, if anywhere,
To hide in our own hollowed dust.
Whatever I gave, I gave no bare
    Pain of a ghost.

I offered, worshiping, that sweet
Cluster of liquors caught in globes,
I burst the riches till they wet
    Your tousled robes;

And though I stole from you no more
Than fireflies gain of the soft moon,
You turned to me, long, long before
    The ghost was gone,

If ghost it was, or melon rind,
Or stag's skeleton hung to dry,
Lover, or song, or only wind
    Sighing your sigh.

A LITTLE GIRL ON HER WAY TO SCHOOL

When the dark dawn humped off to die
The air sang, clearly the country bells
Rang in the light from trees to wells
And silkened every catbird cry.

Webbed in a gown of yellow-white,
Gauzed as a robin where the tree
Blows down over the eyelids, she
Limped on beyond me in the light.

One bell before I woke, the stones
Under the balls of her soft feet
Cried out to her, the leaves in the wet
All tumbled toward her name at once.

And while my waking hung in poise
Between the air and the damp earth,
I saw her startle to the breath
Of birds beginning in her voice.

Be careful of holes, the catbird said,
His nest hanging below her hair,
Nudging the robins windward there,
Whorling the air of glint and shade.

Fall in the hole, the pigeon swore,
His feathers beckoning her to ground,
Burling the sparrows out of sound,
Whorling the glints of shade and air.

Cling to the edge, cling to the edge,
Here, step lightly, touch my beak.
She listened, but she would not speak,
Following the white swan through the hedge.

MY GRANDMOTHER'S GHOST

She skimmed the yellow water like a moth,
Trailing her feet across the shallow stream;
She saw the berries, paused and sampled them
Where a slight spider cleaned his narrow tooth.
Light in the air, she fluttered up the path,
So delicate to shun the leaves and damp,
Like some young wife, holding a slender lamp
To find her stray child, or the moon, or both.

Even before she reached the empty house,
She beat her wings ever so lightly, rose,
Followed a bee where apples blew like snow;
And then, forgetting what she wanted there,
Too full of blossom and green light to care,
She hurried to the ground, and slipped below.

SAINT JUDAS

They answered
and said unto him,
Thou wast altogether born in sin,
and dost thou teach us?
And they
cast him out

TO PHILIP TIMBERLAKE, MY TEACHER
AND TO SONJIA URSETH, MY STUDENT

I stop my habitual thinking, as if the plow had suddenly run deeper in its furrow through the crust of the world. How can I go on, who have just stepped over such a bottomless skylight in the bog of my life? Suddenly old Time winked at me, — Ah you know me, you rogue, — and news had come that IT *was well. . . . Heal yourselves, doctors; by God I live.*

— THOREAU, A Week on the Concord and Merrimack Rivers

I. Lunar Changes

COMPLAINT

She's gone. She was my love, my moon or more.
She chased the chickens out and swept the floor,
Emptied the bones and nut-shells after feasts,
And smacked the kids for leaping up like beasts.
Now morbid boys have grown past awkwardness;
The girls let stitches out, dress after dress,
To free some swinging body's riding space
And form the new child's unimagined face.
Yet, while vague nephews, spitting on their curls,
Amble to pester winds and blowsy girls,
What arm will sweep the room, what hand will hold
New snow against the milk to keep it cold?
And who will dump the garbage, feed the hogs,
And pitch the chickens' heads to hungry dogs?
Not my lost hag who dumbly bore such pain:
Childbirth and midnight sassafras and rain.
New snow against her face and hands she bore,
And now lies down, who was my moon or more.

PAUL

I used to see her in the door,
Lifting up her hand to wave
To citizens, or pass the hour
With neighboring wives who did not have
Anything more than time to say.

I used to see her in the door,
Simple and quiet woman, slim;
And so, I think, Paul cared the more
The night they carried her from him,
The night they carried her away.

The doctor did not even ask
For any neighborly advice;
He knew he had a simple task,
And it was obvious from his eyes
There was not anything to say.

The doctor had a word for Paul;
He said that she was resting now,
And would not wake, and that was all.
And then he walked into the snow,
Into the snow he walked away.

And did Paul shriek and curse the air,
And did he pummel with his fist
Against the wall, or tear his hair
And rush outside to bite the mist
That did not have a thing to say?

He sat upon her ruffled bed
And did not even look at me.
She was lovely, she was dead.
Some sparrows chirruped on a tree
Outside, and then they flew away.

AN OFFERING FOR MR. BLUEHART

That was a place, when I was young,
Where two or three good friends and I
Tested the fruit against the tongue
Or threw the withered windfalls by.
The sparrows, angry in the sky,
Denounced us from a broken bough.
They limp along the wind and die.
The apples all are eaten now.

Behind the orchard, past one hill
The lean satanic owner lay
And threatened us with murder till

We stole his riches all away.
He caught us in the act one day
And damned us to the laughing bone,
And fired his gun across the gray
Autumn where now his life is done.

Sorry for him, or any man
Who lost his labored wealth to thieves,
Today I mourn him, as I can,
By leaving in their golden leaves
Some luscious apples overhead.
Now may my abstinence restore
Peace to the orchard and the dead.
We shall not nag them any more.

OLD MAN DRUNK

He sits before me now, reptilian, cold,
Worn skeletal with sorrow for his child.
He would have lied to her, were he not old:
An old man's fumbling lips are not defiled
By the sweet lies of love. Yet one must be
Skillful to bring it off; that treachery
Whips back to lash the bungler of its art.
He curses his ineptitude of heart.

He knows the quivering eye of youth is blind.
The pale ears, roaring deep as shell, are deaf
To the half-drowning cry of love behind
The skull. His daughter struck him in her grief
Across the face, hearing her lover dead.
He stood behind her chair, he bowed his head,
Knowing that even death cannot prolong
The quick hysteric angers of the young.

I can say nothing. I will see him sit
Under the vacant clock, till I grow old.
The barkeep's wife returns to throw her fit
And pitch us out into the early cold.

I touch his shoulder, but he does not move,
Lost in the blind bewilderment of love,
The meaningless despair that could not keep
His daughter long from falling off to sleep.

Meanwhile, the many faces of old age
Flutter before me in the tavern haze.
He cannot let me see him weep and rage
Into his wrinkled pillow. Face by face,
He grins to entertain, he fills my glass,
Cold to the gestures of my vague *alas,*
Gay as a futile god who cannot die
Till daylight, when the barkeep says goodbye.

SPARROWS IN A HILLSIDE DRIFT

Pitiful dupes of old illusion, lost
And fallen in the white, they glitter still
Sprightly as when they bathed in summer dust,
Then fade among the crystals on the hill.

Lonely for warm days when the season broke,
Alert to wing and fire, they must have flown
To rest among those toughened boughs of oak
That brood above us, now the fire is gone.

Walking around to breathe, I kick aside
The soft brown feather and the brittle beak.
All flesh is fallen snow. The days deride
The wings of these deluded, once they break.

Somewhere the race of wittier birds survive,
Southering slowly with the cooling days.
They pause to quiver in the wind alive
Like some secure felicity of phrase.

But these few blunderers below my hands
Assault the ear with silence on the wind.

I lose their words, though winter understands.
Man is the listener gone deaf and blind.

The oak above us shivers in the bleak
And lucid winter day; and, far below
Our gathering of the cheated and the weak,
A chimney whispers to a cloud of snow.

A NOTE LEFT IN JIMMY LEONARD'S SHACK

Near the dry river's water-mark we found
    Your brother Minnegan,
Flopped like a fish against the muddy ground.
Beany, the kid whose yellow hair turns green,
Told me to find you, even in the rain,
    And tell you he was drowned.

I hid behind the chassis on the bank,
    The wreck of someone's Ford:
I was afraid to come and wake you drunk:
You told me once the waking up was hard,
The daylight beating at you like a board.
    Blood in my stomach sank.

Beside, you told him never to go out
    Along the river-side
Drinking and singing, clattering about.
You might have thrown a rock at me and cried
I was to blame, I let him fall in the road
    And pitch down on his side.

Well, I'll get hell enough when I get home
    For coming up this far,
Leaving the note, and running as I came.
I'll go and tell my father where you are.
You'd better go find Minnegan before
    Policemen hear and come.

Beany went home, and I got sick and ran,
　　You old son of a bitch.
You better hurry down to Minnegan;
He's drunk or dying now, I don't know which,
Rolled in the roots and garbage like a fish,
　　The poor old man.

AT THOMAS HARDY'S BIRTHPLACE, 1953

1

The nurse carried him up the stair
Into his mother's sleeping room.
The beeches lashed the roof and dragged the air
　　Because of storm.

Wind could have overturned the dead.
Moth and beetle and housefly crept
Under the door to find the lamp, and cowered:
　　But still he slept.

The ache and sorrow of darkened earth
Left pathways soft and meadows sodden;
The small Frome overflowed the firth,
　　And he lay hidden

In the arms of the tall woman gone
To soothe his mother during the dark;
Nestled against the awkward flesh and bone
　　When the rain broke.

2

Last night at Stinsford where his heart
Is buried now, the rain came down.
Cold to the hidden joy, the secret hurt,
　　His heart is stone.

But over the dead leaves in the wet
The mouse goes snooping, and the bird.

Something the voiceless earth does not forget
    They come to guard,

Maybe, the heart who would not tell
Whatever secret he learned from the ground,
Who turned aside and heard the human wail,
    That other sound.

More likely, though, the laboring feet
Of fieldmouse, hedgehog, moth and hawk
Seek in the storm what comfort they can get
    Under the rock

Where surely the heart will not wake again
To endure the unending beat of the air,
Having been nursed beyond the sopping rain,
    Back down the stair.

EVENING

I called him to come in,
The wide lawn darkened so.
Laughing, he held his chin
And hid beside a bush.
The light gave him a push,
Shadowy grass moved slow.
He crept on agile toes
Under a sheltering rose.

His mother, still beyond
The bare porch and the door,
Called faintly out of sound,
And vanished with her voice.
I caught his curious eyes
Measuring me, and more —
The light dancing behind
My shoulder in the wind.

Then, struck beyond belief
By the child's voice I heard,
I saw his hair turn leaf,
His dancing toes divide
To hooves on either side,
One hand become a bird.
Startled, I held my tongue
To hear what note he sang.

Where was the boy gone now?
I stood on the grass, alone.
Swung from the apple bough
The bees ignored my cry.
A dog roved past, and I
Turned up a sinking stone,
But found beneath no more
Than grasses dead last year.

Suddenly lost and cold,
I knew the yard lay bare.
I longed to touch and hold
My child, my talking child,
Laughing or tame or wild —
Solid in light and air,
The supple hands, the face
To fill that barren place.

Slowly, the leaves descended,
The birds resolved to hands;
Laugh, and the charm was ended,
The hungry boy stepped forth.
He stood on the hard earth,
Like one who understands
Fairy and ghost—but less
Our human loneliness.

Then, on the withering lawn,
He walked beside my arm.
Trees and the sun were gone,
Everything gone but us.

His mother sang in the house,
And kept our supper warm,
And loved us, God knows how,
The wide earth darkened so.

DOG IN A CORNFIELD

Fallow between the horny trees
    The empty field
Lay underneath the motions of the cloud.
My master called for bobwhites on his knees,
    And suddenly the wind revealed
The body pitching forward in the mud.

My master leaped alive at first,
    And cried, and ran
Faster than air could echo feet and hands.
The lazy maples wailed beyond the crust
    Of earth and artificial man.
Here lay one death the autumn understands.

How could I know he ran to lie,
    And joke with me,
Beside the toppled scarecrow there, as though
His body, like the straw, lay beaten dry?
    Growling, I circled near a tree,
Indifferent to a solitary crow.

Down on the stubble field the pair
    Lay side by side,
Scarecrow and master. I could hardly tell
Body from body, and the color of hair
    Blended, to let my master hide.
His laughter thickened like a droning bell.

I called him out of earth, to come
    And walk with me,
To leave that furrow where the man's shape broke,

To let the earth collapse, and come on home.
    The limber scarecrow knew the way
To meet the wind, that monumental joke;

But once the real man tumbled down,
    Funny or not,
The broomstick and the straw might leap and cry.
Scared of the chance to wrestle wood and stone,
    I howled into the air, forgot
How scarecrows stumble in a field to die.

Snarling, I leaped the rusty fence,
    I ran across
The shock of leaves, blundering as I tore
Into the scarecrow in the man's defense.
    My master rolled away on grass
And saw me scatter legs and arms in air.

And saw me summon all my force
    To shake apart
The brittle shoes, the tough blades of the brains
Back to the ground; the brutal formlessness,
    The twisted knot of its arid heart
Back to the sweet roots of the autumn rains.

Where do the sticks and stones get off,
    Mocking the shape
Of eyes younger than summer, of thoughtful hands?
The real man falls to nothing fast enough.
    I barked into the air, to keep
The man quick to a joy he understands.

ON MINDING ONE'S OWN BUSINESS

Ignorant two, we glide
On ripples near the shore.
The rainbows leap no more,
And men in boats alight
To see the day subside.

All evening fins have drowned
Back in the summer dark.
Above us, up the bank,
Obscure on lonely ground,
A shack receives the night.

I hold the lefthand oar
Out of the wash, and guide
The skiff away so wide
We wander out of sight
As soundless as before.

We will not land to bear
Our will upon that house,
Nor force on any place
Our dull offensive weight.

Somebody may be there,
Peering at us outside
Across the even lake,
Wondering why we take
Our time and stay so late.

Long may the lovers hide
In viny shacks from those
Who thrash among the trees,
Who curse, who have no peace,
Who pitch and moan all night
For fear of someone's joys,
Deploring the human face.

From prudes and muddying fools,
Kind Aphrodite, spare
All hunted criminals,
Hoboes, and whip-poor-wills,
And girls with rumpled hair,
All, all of whom might hide
Within that darkening shack.
Lovers may live, and abide.

Wherefore, I turn my back,
And trawl our boat away,
Lest someone fear to call
A girl's name till we go
Over the lake so slow
We hear the darkness fall.

THE MORALITY OF POETRY
to Gerald Enscoe

Would you the undulation of one wave,
its trick to me transfer. . . .
                                    — WHITMAN

I stood above the sown and generous sea
Late in the day, to muse about your words:
Your human images come to pray for hands
To wipe their vision clear, your human voice
Flinging the poem forward into sound.
Below me, roaring elegies to birds,
Intricate, cold, the waters crawled the sands,
Heaving and groaning, casting up a tree,
A shell, a can to clamber over the ground:
Slow celebration, cluttering ripple on wave.

I wondered when the complicated sea
Would tear and tangle in itself and die,
Sheer outrage hammering itself to death:
Hundreds of gulls descending to the froth,
Their bodies clumped and fallen, lost to me.
Counting those images, I meant to say
A hundred gulls decline to nothingness;
But, high in cloud, a single naked gull
Shadows a depth in heaven for the eye.
And, for the ear, under the wail and snarl
Of groping foghorns and the winds grown old,
A single human word for love of air
Gathers the tangled discords up to song.
Summon the rare word for the rare desire.

60

It thrives on hunger, and it rises strong
To live above the blindness and the noise
Only as long as bones are clean and spare,
The spine exactly set, the muscles lean.
Before you let a single word escape,
Starve it in darkness; lash it to the shape
Of tense wing skimming on the sea alone. . . .

So through my cold lucidity of heart
I thought to send you careful rules of song.
But gulls ensnare me here; the sun fades; thought
By thought the tide heaves, bobbing my words' damp wings;
Mind is the moon-wave roiling on ripples now.
Sun on the bone-hulled galleons of those gulls
Charms my immense irrelevance away,
And lures wings moonward. Openly she soars,
A miracle out of all gray sounds, the moon,
Deepening and rifting swell and formal sky.
Woman or bird, she plumes the ashening sound,
Flaunting to nothingness the rules I made.
Scattering cinders, widening, over the sand
Her cold epistle falls. To plumb the fall
Of silver on ripple, evening ripple on wave,
Quick celebration where she lives for light,
I let all measures die. My voice is gone,
My words to you unfinished, where they lie
Common and bare as stone in diamond veins.
Where the sea moves the word moves, where the sea
Subsides, the slow word fades with lunar tides.
Now still alive, my skeletal words gone bare,
Lapsing like dead gulls' brittle wings and drowned,
In a mindless dance, beneath the darkening air,
I send you shoreward echoes of my voice:
The dithyrambic gestures of the moon,
Sun-lost, the mind plumed, Dionysian,
A blue sea-poem, joy, moon-ripple on wave.

AT THE SLACKENING OF THE TIDE

Today I saw a woman wrapped in rags
Leaping along the beach to curse the sea.
Her child lay floating in the oil, away
From oarlock, gunwale, and the blades of oars.
The skinny lifeguard, raging at the sky,
Vomited sea, and fainted on the sand.

The cold simplicity of evening falls
Dead on my mind,
And underneath the piles the water
Leaps up, leaps up, and sags down slowly, farther
Than seagulls disembodied in the drag
Of oil and foam.

Plucking among the oyster shells a man
Stares at the sea, that stretches on its side.
Now far along the beach, a hungry dog
Announces everything I knew before:
Obliterate naiads weeping underground,
Where Homer's tongue thickens with human howls.

I would do anything to drag myself
Out of this place:
Root up a seaweed from the water,
To stuff it in my mouth, or deafen me,
Free me from all the force of human speech;
Go drown, almost.

Warm in the pleasure of the dawn I came
To sing my song
And look for mollusks in the shallows,
The whorl and coil that pretty up the earth,
While far below us, flaring in the dark,
The stars go out.

What did I do to kill my time today,
After the woman ranted in the cold,
The mellow sea, the sound blown dark as wine?

After the lifeguard rose up from the waves
Like a sea-lizard with the scales washed off?
Sit there, admiring sunlight on a shell?

Abstract with terror of the shell, I stared
Over the waters where
God brooded for the living all one day.
Lonely for weeping, starved for a sound of mourning,
I bowed my head, and heard the sea far off
Washing its hands.

ALL THE BEAUTIFUL ARE BLAMELESS

Out of a dark into the dark she leaped
Lightly this day.
Heavy with prey, the evening skiffs are gone,
And drowsy divers lift their helmets off,
Dry on the shore.

Two stupid harly-charlies got her drunk
And took her swimming naked on the lake.
The waters rippled lute-like round the boat,
And far beyond them, dipping up and down,
Unmythological sylphs, their names unknown,
Beckoned to sandbars where the evenings fall.

Only another drunk would say she heard
A natural voice
Luring the flesh across the water.
I think of those unmythological
Sylphs of the trees.

Slight but orplidean shoulders weave in dusk
Before my eyes when I walk lonely forward
To kick beer-cans from tracked declivities.
If I, being lightly sane, may carve a mouth
Out of the air to kiss, the drowned girl surely
Listened to lute-song where the sylphs are gone.
The living and the dead glide hand in hand

Under cool waters where the days are gone.
Out of the dark into a dark I stand.

The ugly curse the world and pin my arms
Down by their grinning teeth, sneering a blame.
Closing my eyes, I look for hungry swans
To plunder the lake and bear the girl away,
Back to the larger waters where the sea
Sifts, judges, gathers the body, and subsides.

But here the starved, touristic crowd divides
And offers the dead
Hell for the living body's evil:
The girl flopped in the water like a pig
And drowned dead drunk.

So do the pure defend themselves. But she,
Risen to kiss the sky, her limbs still whole,
Rides on the dark tarpaulin toward the shore;
And the hired saviours turn their painted shell
Along the wharf, to list her human name.
But the dead have no names, they lie so still,
And all the beautiful are blameless now.

IN A VIENNESE CEMETERY

There Hugo Wolf is buried: fully formed
Out of the stone a naked woman leans
Kissing the uncut stone, the solid void
Of granite cold to sound and song unmade.
She holds her body to the rock, unwarmed
By any sculptor's trick. The climbing vines
Fail to relieve what barren death destroyed:
The life half over, and the song gone dead.

Somewhere unborn inside the stone a mouth
Hungered severely for her starving kiss.
Reaching his lover's hands across the dark,

64

Maybe the dead musician underneath
Whispers to touch the woman's nakedness,
To strike a fire inside the yearning rock.

Brush aside that fantasy, I feel
The wind of early autumn cross the ground,
I turn among the stones to let it blow
Clearly across my face as over stone.
Bodiless yearnings make no music fall;
Breath of the body bears the living sound.
This dour musician died so long ago
Even his granite beard is softened down.

An age or so will wear away his grave,
The lover who attains the girl be rain,
The granite underneath be carved no more.
Only the living body calls up love,
That shadow risen casually from stone
To clothe the nakedness of bare desire.

A PRAYER IN MY SICKNESS
la muerte entra y sale

You hear the long roll of the plunging ground,
The whistle of stones, the quail's cry in the grass.
I stammer like a bird, I rasp like stone,
I mutter, with gray hands upon my face.
The earth blurs, beyond me, into dark.
Spinning in such bewildered sleep, I need
To know you, whirring above me, when I wake.
Come down. Come down. I lie afraid.
I have lain alien in my self so long,
How can I understand love's angry tongue?

THE COLD DIVINITIES

I should have been delighted there to hear
The woman and the boy,

Singing along the shore together.
Lightly the shawl and shoulder of the sea
Upbore the plume and body of one gull
Dropping his lines.

Loping behind a stone too large for waves
To welter down like pumice without sound,
Laughing his languages awake, that boy
Flung to his mother, on a wrack of weeds,
Delicate words, a whisper like a spume
Fluting along the edges of the shore.

I should have been delighted that the cries
Of fishermen and gulls
Faded among the swells, to let me
Gather into the fine seines of my ears
The frail fins of their voices as they sang:
My wife and child.

Lovely the mother shook her hair, so long
And glittering in its darkness, as the moon
In the deep lily-heart of the hollowing swells
Flamed toward the cold caves of the evening sea:
And the fine living frieze of her Greek face;
The sea behind her, fading, and the sails.

I should have been delighted for the gaze,
The billowing of the girl,
The bodying skirt, the ribbons falling;
I should have run to gather in my arms
The mother and the child who seemed to live
Stronger than stone and wave.

But slowly twilight gathered up the skiffs
Into its long gray arms; and though the sea
Grew kind as possible to wrack-splayed birds;
And though the sea like woman vaguely wept;
She could not hide her clear enduring face,
Her cold divinities of death and change.

66

THE REVELATION

Stress of his anger set me back
To musing over time and space.
The apple branches dripping black
Divided light across his face.
Towering beneath the broken tree,
He seemed a stony shade to me.
He spoke no language I could hear
For long with my distracted ear.

Between his lips and my delight
In blowing wind, a bird-song rose.
And soon in fierce, blockading light
The planet's shadow hid his face.
And all that strongly molded bone
Of chest and shoulder soon were gone,
Devoured among the solid shade.
Assured his angry voice was dead,

And satisfied his judging eyes
Had given over plaguing me,
I stood to let the darkness rise —
My darkness, gathering in the tree,
The field, the swollen shock of hay,
Bank of the creek half washed away.
Lost in my self, and unaware
Of love, I took the evening air.

I blighted, for a moment's length,
My father out of sight and sound;
Prayed to annihilate his strength,
The proud legs planted on the ground.
Why should I hear his angry cry
Or bear the damning of his eye?
Anger for anger I could give,
And murder for my right to live.

The moon rose. Lucidly the moon
Ran skimming shadows off the trees.

To strip all shadow but its own
Down to the perfect mindlessness.
Yet suddenly the moonlight caught
My father's finger's reaching out,
The strong arm begging me for love,
Loneliness I knew nothing of.

And weeping in the nakedness
Of moonlight and of agony,
His blue eyes lost their barrenness
And bore a blossom out to me.
And as I ran to give it back,
The apple branches, dripping black,
Trembled across the lunar air
And dropped white petals on his hair.

A WINTER DAY IN OHIO
P. W. T. died in late Spring, 1957

Clever, defensive, seasoned animals
Plato and Christ deny your grave. But man,
Who slept for years alone, will turn his face
Alone to the common wall before his time.
Between the woodchuck and the cross, alone
All afternoon, I take my time to mourn.
I am too cold to cry against the snow
Of roots and stars, drifting above your face.

II. A Sequence of Love Poems

Thou know'st, the first time that we smell the air
We wawl and cry.
                                    — King Lear

A BREATH OF AIR

I walked, when love was gone,
Out of the human town,
For an easy breath of air.
Beyond a break in the trees,
Beyond the hangdog lives
Of old men, beyond girls:
The tall stars held their peace.
Looking in vain for lies
I turned, like earth, to go.
An owl's wings hovered, bare
On the moon's hills of snow.

And things were as they were.

IN SHAME AND HUMILIATION

He will launch a curse upon the world, and as only man can curse (it is his privilege,
the primary distinction between him and other animals), maybe by his curse alone he
will attain his object — that is, convince himself that he is a man and not a piano-key!
                                    — DOSTOYEVSKY, *Notes from Underground*

What can a man do that a beast cannot,
A bird, a reptile, any fiercer thing?
    He can amaze the ground
With anger never hissed in a snake's throat
    Or past a bitch's fang,
Though, suffocate, he cannot make a sound.

He can out-rage the forked tongue with a word,
The iron forged of his pain, over and over,

Till the cold blade can fall
And beak an enemy's heart quick as a bird,
    And then retire to cover,
To vines of hair, declivities of skull.

Outright the snake, faster than man, can kill.
A mongrel's teeth can snarl as man's cannot.
    And a bird, unbodied soul
Soaring and dazzling, in the cloud at will
    Outbeautifies the flight
Of halt man's clavicles that flop and wheel.

Their cries last longer. Sinew of wing and coil,
Or sprung thighs of hounds impinge their iron
    Easy and quick, to leap
Over the brooks, the miles and days, like oil
    Flung on a surge of green.
A man limps into nothing more than sleep.

But under the dream he always dreams too late,
That stark abounding dream of wretchedness
    Where stones and very trees
Ignore his name, and crows humiliate,
    And fiends below the face,
Serpents, women, and dogs dance to deny his face —

He will not deny, he will not deny his own.
Thrashing in lakes or pools of broken glass,
    He hunches over to look
And feel his mouth, his nostrils, feel of the bone,
    A man's ultimate face:
The individual bone, that burns like ice.

That fire, that searing cold is what I claim:
What makes me man, that dogs can never share,
    Woman or brilliant bird,
The beaks that mock but cannot speak the names
    Of the blind rocks, of the stars.
Sprawling in dark, I burn my sudden pride.

70

Let my veins wither now, my words revolt
Serpent or bird or pure untroubled mind.
    I will avow my face
Unto my face and, through the spirit's vault,
    Deliberate underground,
Devour the locusts of my bitterness.

That angel, wheeled upon my heart, survives,
Nourished by food the righteous cannot eat
    And loathe to move among.
They die, fastidious, while the spirit thrives
    Out of its own defeat.
The pure, the pure! will never live so long.

THE ACCUSATION

I kissed you in the dead of dark,
And no one knew, or wished to know,
You bore, across your face, a mark
From birth, those shattered years ago.
Now I can never keep in mind
The memory of your ugliness
At a clear moment. Now my blind
Fingers alone can read your face.

Often enough I had seen that slash
Of fire you quickly hid in shame;
You flung your scarf across the flesh,
And turned away, and said my name.
Thus I remember daylight and
The scar that made me pity you.
God damn them both, you understand.
Pity can scar love's face, I know.

I loved your face because your face
Was broken. When my hands were heavy,
You kissed me only in a darkness
To make me daydream you were lovely.
All the lovely emptiness

On earth is easy enough to find.
You had no right to turn your face
From me. Only the truth is kind.

I cannot dream of you by night.
I half-remember what you were.
And I remember the cold daylight,
And pity your disgusting scar
As any light-eyed fool could pity,
Who sees you walking down the street.
I lose your stark essential beauty,
I dream some face I read about.

If I were given a blind god's power
To turn your daylight on again,
I would not raise you smooth and pure:
I would bare to heaven your uncommon pain,
Your scar I had a right to hold,
To look on, for the pain was yours.
Now you are dead, and I grow old,
And the doves cackle out of doors,

And lovers, flicking on the lights,
Turn to behold each lovely other.
Let them remember fair delights.
How can I ever love another?
You had no right to banish me
From that scarred truth of wretchedness,
Your face, that I shall never see
Again, though I search every place.

THE GHOST

I cannot live nor die.
Now shadows rise nor fall,
Whisper aloud nor weep.
Struck beyond time and change
To a claw, a withering thigh,

A breath, a slackening call
To cold throats out of range,
I fade to a broken hope.

What good may mourning do,
The sigh, the soft lament,
The poised turning away
To name one faded name?
I will not name it now.
The day, the heart lie spent.
I find, now that I came,
Love that I cannot say.

The wind builds hock and tongue
Up from the sinewy ground.
But how may the blind air tell
A gnat from a lark? Alone,
Weighed by the laboring sound
Of wind on muscle and hair,
White as a thistle and bare,
I close the gate of hell.

Neat, shallow, hell is here,
Here, where I speak to lips
At one with stone and me,
Living and dead at one:
Love's cry, the shock of fear,
The shadow of rain that drips,
A mirror of gleaming stone,
The hands that cannot see,

Ears stricken blind, and eyes
That cannot speak nor sing,
And arms that barely breathe
Above ground or below.
Lumbering from hell, I gaze
Down at the earth so long,
I need no further go.
Here is the gate of wreath.

Love need no further go
Than back to the earth, to die.
The living need not seek
For love but underfoot.
The first star rises slow
And brambles lash my eye
And lichens trip my foot,
And yet, I cannot speak.

I will stand here, till dawn.
I will not fall down, to pray.
Dark bells may summon you
Out of your dream to cry.
Then I will tread your lawn
Through a soft break of day,
To see your day go by,
Who stare, and stare me through.

THE ALARM

When I came back from my last dream, when I
Whirled in the morning snowfall up the lawn,
I looked behind me where my wings were gone.
Rusting above the snow, for lack of care,
A pile of rakes and shovels rotted away.
Tools of the world were crumbling into air,
And I, neither the living nor the dead,
Paused in the dusk of dawn to wonder why
Any man clambers upward out of shade
To rake and shovel all his dust away.

I found my body sprawled against the bed.
One hand flopped back as though to ward away
Shovels of light. The body wakes to burial:
But my face rebelled; the lids and lips were gray,
And spiders climbed their webs above my head.
I stood above my wreck of flesh and skull:
A foot reclined over the wrenching thigh,
And suddenly, before I joined my face,

74

The eyelids opened, and it stared across
The window pane, into the empty sky.

Neither the living nor the dead I stood,
Longing to leave my poor flesh huddled there
Heaped up for burning under the last laments.
I moved, to leap on spider webs and climb.
But where do spiders fling those filaments,
Those pure formalities of blood and air,
Both perfect and alive? I did no good.
The hands of daylight hammered down my ghost,
And I was home now, bowing into my dust,
To quicken into stupor one more time,
One of the living buried like the dead.

A GIRL WALKING INTO A SHADOW

The mere trees cast no coolness where you go.
Your small feet press no darkness into the grass.
I know your weight of days, and mourn I know.
All hues beneath the ground are bare grayness.

When I was young, I might have touched your hair,
Gestured my warning, how that fire will gray,
Slight arms and delicate hands fall heavier,
And pale feet hasten to a dark delay.

Now old, I love you slowly, through my sound.
Lightly alive, you cannot mourn for trees.
You cannot care how grass, above the gound,
Gathers to mold your shadow's quick caress.

Heavy for you, I hear the futile speech
Of air in trees, of shadows in your hair.
Quick to go by me now, beyond my reach,
You pause. With darkness deepening everywhere,

Something of light falls, pitiful and kind.
Something of love forgot the dark embrace

Of evening, where the lover's eyes go blind
With dreaming on the hollows of your face.

BUT ONLY MINE

I dreamed that I was dead, as all men do,
And feared the dream, though hardly for the sake
Of any thrust of pain my flesh might take
Below the softening shales. Bereft of you,
I lay for days and days alone, I knew
Somewhere above me boughs were burning gold,
And women's frocks were loose, and men grew old.

Grew old. And shrivelled. Asked the time of day.
And then forgot. Turned. Looked among the grass.
Tripped on a twig. Frightened some leaves away.
Children. And girls. I knew, above my face,
Rabbit and jay flocked, wondering how to cross
An empty field stripped naked to the sun.
They halted into a shadow, huddled down.

Rabbit and jay, old man, and girl, and child,
All moved above me, dreaming of broad light.
I heard you walking through the empty field.
Startled awake, I found my living sight:
The grave drifted away, and it was night,
I felt your soft despondent shoulders near.
Out of my dream, the dead rose everywhere.

I did not dream your death, but only mine.

III. The Part Nearest Home

From the uttermost part of the earth have we heard songs,
even glory to the righteous. But I said, My leanness, my
leanness, woe unto me.

— Isaiah, 24:16

WHAT THE EARTH ASKED ME

"Why did you kiss the girl who cried
For lovers through her lonely mind,
Homely as sin and sick of pride?"

    In pity for my kind.

"What good will pity do the lost
Who flutter in the driven wind,
Wild for the body, ghost on ghost?"

    No good, no good to me.

"Why did you hammer with your fist
That beetle on the window-blind,
Withered in summer's holocaust?"

    In pity for my kind.

"What good will pity do the found
Who flutter in the driven wind,
Wild to be ghosts below the ground?"

    No good, no good to me.

"The living and the dead together
Flutter before, flutter behind.
Why do you try to change the weather?"

    In pity for my kind.

"What good will pity do the kiss
That shrivels on the mouth of grief?
Have you been calling me for this?"

No good to me, no good to me.

THE REFUSAL

When we get back, the wagon will be gone,
The porchlight empty in the wind, no doubt;
     And everybody here,
Who damned us for the conscience of a stone,
     Will tell us to get out
And do our sniffling in the dark somewhere.

It may not be delight to hear that word,
The pride of mourners mocking in our faces.
     I offer no delight,
Neither a soft life, nor a grave deferred.
     I have known other places
Ugly as this, and shut them from my sight.

Inside the house, somebody we could love,
Who labored for us till the taut string gave,
     Stares from a half-closed eye.
Why should we gaze back in that pit of love?
     All the beloved lie
In the perpetual savagery of graves.

Come here to me; I will not let you go
To suffer on some relative's hard shoulder —
     Weeping woman or man.
God, I have died so many days ago,
     The funeral began
When I was born, and will go on forever: —

Unless I shut the door myself, and take
Your elbow, drag you bodily, out of breath
     And let the house grow dark.

Inside, that lamentation for the sake
　　Of numbers on a rock
Starves me and freezes you, and kills us both.

Must we reel with the wine of mourning like a drunk?
Look there, the doors are latched, the windows close,
　　And we are told to go.
When we come back, the granite will be sunk
　　An inch or more below
The careful fingers of the healing snows.

Preacher and undertaker follow the cars;
They claimed the comfort of the earth, and lied.
　　Better to trust the moon
Blown in the soft bewilderment of stars;
　　The living lean on pain,
The hard stones of the earth are on our side.

AMERICAN TWILIGHTS, 1957

　to Caryl Chessman

I
The buckles glitter, billies lean
Supple and cold as men on walls.
The trusties' faces, yawning green,
Summon up heart, as someone calls
For light, for light! and evening falls.

Checking the cells, the warden piles
Shadow on shadow where he goes
Beyond the catwalk, down the files,
Sneering at one who thumbs his nose.
One weeps, and stumbles on his toes.

Tear and tormented snicker and heart
Click in the darkness; close, and fade.
Clean locks together mesh and part,

And lonely lifers, foot and head,
Huddle against the bed they made.

2
Lie dark, beloved country, now.
Trouble no dream, so still you lie.
Citizens drawl their dreams away;
Stupored, they hid their agony
Deep in the rock; but men must die.

Tall on the earth I would have sung
Heroes of hell, could I have learned
Their names to marvel on my tongue;
The land is dark where they have turned,
And now their very names are burned.

But buried under trestled rock
The broken thief and killer quake:
Tower by tower and clock by clock
Citizens wind the towns asleep.
God, God have pity when they wake.

Haunted by gallows, peering in dark,
I conjure prisons out of wet
And strangling pillows where I mark
The misery man must not forget,
Though I have found no prison yet.

Lo now, the desolation man
Has tossed away like a gnawed bone
Will hunt him where the sea began,
Summon him out of tree and stone,
Damn him, before his dream be gone: —

Seek him behind his bars, to crack
Out the dried kernel of his heart.
God, God have pity if he wake,
Have mercy on man who dreamed apart.
God, God have pity on man apart.

DEVOTIONS

I longed to kill you once, when I was young,
Because you laughed at me before my friends.
    And now the baffled prose
Of a belated vengeance numbs my tongue.
    Come back, before the last wind bends
Your body to the void beyond repose.

Standing alone before your grave, I read
The name, the season, every decent praise
    A chisel might devise —
Deliberate scrawls to guard us from the dead.
    And yet I lift my strength, to raise
Out of the mossy wallow your pig's eyes.

The summons fell, but I could not come home
To gloat above the hackling and the rasp
    Caught in your corded throat;
And, many towns away, I heard your doom
    Tolling the hate beyond my grasp,
Thieving the poisons of my angry thought.

After so many years to lose the vision
Of your last anguish! Furious at the cheat,
    After your burial
I traveled here, to lay my weak derision
    Fresh as a garland at your feet.
All day I have gathered curses, but they fail.

I cannot even call to mind so clearly,
As once I could, your confident thin voice
    Banishing me to nothing.
Your hand crumbles, your sniffing nostrils barely
    Evoke the muscles of my loathing;
And I too die, who came here to rejoice.

Lost mocker of my childhood, how the moss
Softens your hair, how deeply nibbling fangs
    Sink in the careless ground.

Seasons of healing grasses weave across
　　Your caving lips, and dull my strange
Terror of failures. Shaken, I have found

Nothing to mark you off in earth but stone.
Walking here lonely and strange now, I must find
　　A grave to prod my wrath
Back to its just devotions. Miserable bone,
　　Devouring jaw-hinge, glare gone blind,
Come back, be damned of me, your aftermath.

AT THE EXECUTED MURDERER'S GRAVE
(for J. L. D.)

*Why should we do this? What good is it to us? Above all, how
can we do such a thing? How can it possibly be done?*

　　　　　　　　　　　　　　　　　— FREUD

1

My name is James A. Wright, and I was born
Twenty-five miles from this infected grave,
In Martins Ferry, Ohio, where one slave
To Hazel-Atlas Glass became my father.
He tried to teach me kindness. I return
Only in memory now, aloof, unhurried,
To dead Ohio, where I might lie buried,
Had I not run away before my time.
Ohio caught George Doty. Clean as lime,
His skull rots empty here. Dying's the best
Of all the arts men learn in a dead place.
I walked here once. I made my loud display,
Leaning for language on a dead man's voice.
Now sick of lies, I turn to face the past.
I add my easy grievance to the rest:

2

Doty, if I confess I do not love you,
Will you let me alone? I burn for my own lies.
The nights electrocute my fugitive,

My mind. I run like the bewildered mad
At St. Clair Sanitarium, who lurk,
Arch and cunning, under the maple trees,
Pleased to be playing guilty after dark.
Staring to bed, they croon self-lullabies.
Doty, you make me sick. I am not dead.
I croon my tears at fifty cents per line.

3
Idiot, he demanded love from girls,
And murdered one. Also, he was a thief.
He left two women, and a ghost with child.
The hair, foul as a dog's upon his head,
Made such revolting Ohio animals
Fitter for vomit than a kind man's grief.
I waste no pity on the dead that stink,
And no love's lost between me and the crying
Drunks of Belaire, Ohio, where police
Kick at their kidneys till they die of drink.
Christ may restore them whole, for all of me.
Alive and dead, those giggling muckers who
Saddled my nightmares thirty years ago
Can do without my widely printed sighing
Over their pains with paid sincerity.
I do not pity the dead, I pity the dying.

4
I pity myself, because a man is dead.
If Belmont County killed him, what of me?
His victims never loved him. Why should we?
And yet, nobody had to kill him either.
It does no good to woo the grass, to veil
The quicklime hole of a man's defeat and shame.
Nature-lovers are gone. To hell with them.
I kick the clods away, and speak my name.

5
This grave's gash festers. Maybe it will heal,
When all are caught with what they had to do
In fear of love, when every man stands still

By the last sea,
And the princes of the sea come down
To lay away their robes, to judge the earth
And its dead, and we dead stand undefended everywhere,
And my bodies — father and child and unskilled criminal —
Ridiculously kneel to bare my scars,
My sneaking crimes, to God's unpitying stars.

6

Staring politely, they will not mark my face
From any murderer's, buried in this place.
Why should they? We are nothing but a man.

7

Doty, the rapist and the murderer,
Sleeps in a ditch of fire, and cannot hear;
And where, in earth or hell's unholy peace,
Men's suicides will stop, God knows, not I.
Angels and pebbles mock me under trees.
Earth is a door I cannot even face.
Order be damned, I do not want to die,
Even to keep Belaire, Ohio, safe.
The hackles on my neck are fear, not grief.
(Open, dungeon! Open, roof of the ground!)
I hear the last sea in the Ohio grass,
Heaving a tide of gray disastrousness.
Wrinkles of winter ditch the rotted face
Of Doty, killer, imbecile, and thief:
Dirt of my flesh, defeated, underground.

SAINT JUDAS

When I went out to kill myself, I caught
A pack of hoodlums beating up a man.
Running to spare his suffering, I forgot
My name, my number, how my day began,
How soldiers milled around the garden stone
And sang amusing songs; how all that day

84

Their javelins measured crowds; how I alone
Bargained the proper coins, and slipped away.

Banished from heaven, I found this victim beaten,
Stripped, kneed, and left to cry. Dropping my rope
Aside, I ran, ignored the uniforms:
Then I remembered bread my flesh had eaten,
The kiss that ate my flesh. Flayed without hope,
I held the man for nothing in my arms.

SOME TRANSLATIONS

TEN SHORT POEMS
(from the Spanish of Juan Ramón Jiménez)

1. Rose of the Sea
The white moon takes the sea away from the sea
and gives it back to the sea. Beautiful,
conquering by means of the pure and tranquil,
the moon compels the truth to delude itself
that it is truth become whole, eternal, solitary,
though it is not so.
                    Yes.
                            Divine plainness,
you pierce the familiar certainty, you place
a new soul into whatever is real.
Unpredictable rose! you took the rose away
from the rose, and you could give back
the rose to the rose.

                                    from *Diario de Poeta y Mar*

2.
To the bridge of love,
old stone between tall cliffs
    — eternal meeting place, red evening —,
I come with my heart.
    — My beloved is only water,
that always passes away, and does not deceive,
that always passes away, and does not change,
that always passes away, and does not end.

                                    from *Eternidades*

3.
The dawn brings with it
that sadness of arriving, by train,
at a station that is not one's own.
    How disagreeable, those rumblings
of a new day that one knows cannot last long —
    — Oh my life! —
Overhead, as the day breaks, a child is crying.

                                    from *Eternidades*

4. Rosebushes
It is the sea, in the earth.
Colors of the south, in the winter sun,
contain the noisy shiftings
of the sea and the coasts . . .
Tomorrow in the sea! — I say, rather, in the earth
that moves, now, into the sea!

from Diario de Poeta y Mar

5. Dreaming
   — No, no!
       and the dirtyneck boy starts crying and running
without getting away, in a moment, on the streets.
       His hands,
he's got something in his hands!
He doesn't know what it is, but he runs to the dawn
With his hidden prize.
Endlessly beforehand, we know what his trophy is:
something ignored, that the soul keeps awake in us.
We almost start to glitter inside his gold
with extravagant nakedness . . .
   — No, no!
       and the dirtyneck boy starts crying and running
without getting away, in a moment, on the street.
The arm is strong, it could easily grab him . . .
The heart, also a beggar, lets him go.

from Diario de Poeta y Mar

6.
How close to becoming spirit something is,
when it is still so immensely far away
from hands!
       like starlight,
like a nameless voice
in a dream, like faraway horses,
that we hear, as we breathe heavily,
one ear placed to the ground;
like the sea on the telephone . . .
And life begins to grow

within us, the delightful daylight
that cannot be switched off,
that is thinning, now, somewhere else.
Ah, how lovely, how lovely,
truth, even if it is not real, how lovely!

from *Diario de Poeta y Mar*

7. On the City Ramparts of Cádiz
The sea is enormous,
just as everything is,
yet it seems to me I am still with you . . .
Soon only water will separate us,
water, restlessly shifting,
water, only water!

from *Diario de Poeta y Mar*

8.
Stormclouds
give their morose faces to the sea.

The water, worked up out of iron,
is a hard, flat landscape,
of exhausted mines,
in a state of collapse,
ruins.

Nothingness! That word, for me,
here, today, comes home,
the cadaver of a word,
laid out, naturally,
in its own grave.
Nothingness!

from *Diario de Poeta y Mar*

9. Moguer
Moguer. Mother and brothers.
The house, clean and warm.
What sunlight there is, what rest
In the whitening cemetery!
In a moment, love grows remote.

The sea does not exist; the field
of vineyards, reddish and level,
is the world, like a bright light shining on nothing.
and flimsy, like a bright light shining on nothing.

Here I have been cheated enough!
Here, the only healthy thing to do is die.
This is the way out, that I wanted so badly,
that escapes into the sunset.

Moguer.   If only I could rise up, sanctified!
Moguer.   Brothers and sisters.

from *Diario de Poeta y Mar*

10.   Life
What I used to regard as a glory shut in my face,
Was a door, opening
toward this clarity:
                    Country without a name:

Nothing can destroy it, this road
of doors, opening, one after another,
always toward reality:
                    Life without calculation!

from *Eternidades*

I WANT TO SLEEP
(from the Spanish of Jorge Guillén)

I shall be still stronger,
Still clearer, purer, so let
The sweet invasion of oblivion come on.
I want to sleep.

If I could forget myself, if I were only
A tranquil tree,
Branches to spread out the silence,
Trunk of mercy.

92

The great darkness, grown motherly,
Deepens little by little,
Brooding over this body that the soul —
After a pause — surrenders.

It may even embark from the endless world,
From its accidents,
And, scattering into stars at the last,
The soul will be daybreak.

Abandoning myself to my accomplice,
My boat,
I shall reach on my ripples and mists
Into the dawn.

I do not want to dream of useless phantoms,
I do not want a cave.
Let the huge moonless spaces
Hold me apart, and defend me.

Let me enjoy so much harmony
Thanks to the ignorance
Of this being, that is so secure
It pretends to be nothing.

Night with its darkness, solitude with its peace,
Everything favors
My delight in the emptiness
That soon will come.

Emptiness, O paradise
Rumored about so long:
Sleeping, sleeping, growing alone
Very slowly.

Darken me, erase me,
Blessed sleep,
As I lie under a heaven that mounts
Its guard over me.

Earth, with your darker burdens,
Drag me back down,
Sink my being into my being:
Sleep, sleep.

NATURE ALIVE
(from the Spanish of Jorge Guillén)

The panel board of the table,
That smooth plane precisely
True to a hair, holds up
Its level form, sustained

By an idea: pure, exact,
The mind's image before
The mind's eyes! And yet,
Full assurance needs the touch

That explores and discovers
How the formal idea sags back
Down to the rich heaviness
Of kindling, trunk and timber

Of walnut. The walnut wood,
Secure in its own whorls
And grains, assured of its long
Season of so much strength

Now fused into the heart
Of this quiet vigor, the stuff
Of a table board, remains
Always, always wild!

LOVE SONG TO A MORNING
(from the Spanish of Jorge Guillén)

Morning, clear morning,
If only I were your lover!

With every step I take on your margin,
I should long for you all the more.

My word hurries to gather
All of your fresh beauty.

Here we are, on our path.
Let me understand you.

Loveliness, held lightly
To the blade of nothingness!

The blue rosemary
Smells of the real earth.

How much of the world does the mallow
Grasp from her stone?

The cricket trills endlessly.
I bow to his patience.

How much joy the honeybee
Leaves to the flower!

And he plunges, laboring
In the heat of the mine.

Now the cricket is hurrying
His song. Is there yet more spring?

Whoever loses all this, loses himself.
So much green, and the field mine!

Heaven that the eye cannot fathom:
It is love that wins you.

Don't I deserve such a morning?
My heart earns it.

Clarity, uttermost strength:
My soul is fulfilled in you.

SOME BEASTS
(from the Spanish of Pablo Neruda)

It was the twilight of the iguana.
From the rainbow-arch of the battlements,
his long tongue like a lance
sank down in the green leaves,
and a swarm of ants, monks with feet chanting,
crawled off into the jungle;
the guanaco, thin as oxygen
in the wide peaks of cloud,
went along, wearing his shoes of gold,
while the llama opened his honest eyes
on the breakable neatness
of a world full of dew.
The monkeys braided a sexual
thread that went on and on
along the shores of the dawn,
demolishing walls of pollen
and startling the butterflies of Muzo
into flying violets.
It was the night of the alligators,
the pure night, crawling
with snouts emerging from ooze,
and out of the sleepy marshes
the confused noise of scaly plates
returned to the ground where they began.

The jaguar brushes the leaves
with a luminous absence,
the puma runs through the branches
like a forest fire,
while the jungle's drunken eyes
burn from inside him.
The badgers scratch the river's
feet, scenting the nest

whose throbbing delicacy
they attack with red teeth.

And deep in the huge waters
the enormous anaconda lies
like the circle around the earth,
covered with ceremonies of mud,
devouring, religious.

THE HEIGHTS OF MACCHU PICCHU, III
(from the Spanish of Pablo Neruda)

The human soul was threshed out like maize in the endless
granary of defeated actions, of mean things that happened,
to the very edge of endurance, and beyond,
and not only death, but many deaths, came to each one:
each day a tiny death, dust, worm, a light
flicked off in the mud at the city's edge, a tiny death
    with coarse wings
pierced into each man like a short lance
and the man was besieged by the bread or by the knife,
the cattle-dealer: the child of sea-harbors, or the dark
    captain of the plough,
or the rag-picker of snarled streets:

everybody lost heart, anxiously waiting for death, the
    short death of every day:
and the grinding bad luck of every day was
like a black cup that they drank, with their hands shaking.

TRUMPETS
(from the German of Georg Trakl)

Under the trimmed willows, where brown children
    are playing
And leaves tumbling, the trumpets blow. A quaking
    of cemeteries.

Banners of scarlet rattle through a sadness of maple
    trees,
Riders along rye-fields, empty mills.

Or shepherds sing during the night, and stags step
    delicately
Into the circle of their fire, the grove's sorrow
    immensely old,
Dancing, they loom up from one black wall;
Banners of scarlet, laughter, insanity, trumpets.

DE PROFUNDIS
(from the German of George Trakl)

It is a stubble field, where a black rain is falling.
It is a brown tree, that stands alone.
It is a hissing wind, that encircles empty houses.
How melancholy the evening is.

Beyond the village,
The soft orphan garners the sparse ears of corn.
Her eyes graze, round and golden, in the twilight
And her womb awaits the heavenly bridegroom.

On the way home
The shepherd found the sweet body
Decayed in a bush of thorns.

I am a shadow far from darkening villages.
I drank the silence of God
Out of the stream in the trees.

Cold metal walks on my forehead.
Spiders search for my heart.
It is a light that goes out in my mouth.

At night, I found myself in a pasture,
Covered with rubbish and the dust of stars.

In a hazel thicket
Angels of crystal rang out once more.

THE RATS
(from the German of Georg Trakl)

In the farmyard the white moon of autumn shines.
Fantastic shadows fall from the eaves of the roof.
A silence is living in the empty windows;
Now from it the rats emerge softly

And skitter here and there, squeaking.
And a gray malodorous mist from the latrine
Follows behind them, sniffing:
Through the mist the ghostly moonlight quivers.

And the rats squeak eagerly as if insane
And go out to fill houses and barns
Which are filled full of fruit and grain.
Icy winds quarrel in the darkness.

A WINTER NIGHT
(from the German of Georg Trakl)

It has been snowing. Past midnight, drunk on purple wine, you leave
the gloomy shelters of men, and the red fire of their fireplaces. Oh the
darkness of night.

Black frost. The ground is hard, the air has a bitter taste. Your stars
make unlucky figures.

With a stiff walk, you tramp along the railroad embankment with huge
eyes, like a soldier charging a dark machinegun nest. Onward!

Bitter snow and moon.

A red wolf, that an angel is strangling. Your trouser legs rustle, as you
walk, like blue ice, and a smile full of suffering and pride petrifies your face,

and your forehead is white before the ripe desire of the frost;

or else it bends down silently over the doze of the nightwatchman, slumped down in his wooden shack.

Frost and smoke. A white shirt of stars burns on your clothed shoulders, and the hawk of God strips flesh out of your hard heart.

Oh the stony hill. The cool body, forgotten and silent, is melting away in the silver snow.

Sleep is black. For a long time the ear follows the motion of the stars deep down in the ice.

When you woke, the churchbells were ringing in the town. Out of the door in the east the rose-colored day walked with silver light.

SLEEP
(from the German of Georg Trakl)

Not your dark poisons again,
White sleep!
This fantastically strange garden
Of trees in deepening twilight
Fills up with serpents, nightmoths,
Spiders, bats.
Approaching the stranger! Your abandoned shadow
In the red of evening
Is a dark pirate ship
On the salty oceans of confusion.
White birds from the outskirts of the night
Flutter out over the shuddering cities
Of steel.

I AM FREED
(from the Spanish of César Vallejo)

I am freed from the burdens of the sea

when the waters come toward me.

Let us always sail out. Let us taste
the marvellous song, the song spoken
by the lower lips of desire.
Oh beautiful virginity.
The saltless breeze passes.

From the distance, I breathe marrows,
hearing the profound score, as the surf
hunts for its keys.

And if we banged
into the absurd,
We shall cover ourselves with the gold of owning
        nothing,
and hatch the still unborn wing
of the night, sister
of the orphaned wing of the day,
that is not really a wing since it is only one.

WHITE ROSE
(from the Spanish of César Vallejo)

I feel all right. Now
a stoical frost shines
in me.
It makes me laugh, this ruby-colored
rope
that creaks in my body.

Endless rope,
like a spiral
descending
from
evil . . .
rope, bloody and clumsy,
shaped by
a thousand waiting daggers.

Because it goes in this way, braiding
its rolls of funeral crepe,
and because it ties the quivering cat
of Fear to the frozen nest,
to the final fire.

Now surrounded by light
I am calm.
And out on my Pacific
a shipwrecked coffin mews.

A DIVINE FALLING OF LEAVES
(from the Spanish of César Vallejo)

Moon: royal crown of an enormous head,
dropping leaves into yellow shadows as you go.
Red crown of a Jesus who broods
tragically, softly over emeralds!

Moon: reckless heart in heaven,
why do you row toward the west
in that cup filled with blue wine,
whose hull is defeated and sad?

Moon: it is no use flying anyway,
so you go up in a flame of scattered opals:
maybe you are my heart, who is like a gypsy,
who loafs in the sky, shedding poems like tears! . . .

OUR DAILY BREAD
(from the Spanish of César Vallejo)

(for Alejandro Gamboa)

Breakfast is drunk down . . . Damp earth
of the cemetery gives off the fragrance of the
        precious blood.
City of winter . . . the mordant crusade

of a cart that seems to pull behind it
an emotion of fasting that cannot get free!

I wish I could beat on all the doors,
and ask for somebody; and then
look at the poor, and, while they wept softly,
give bits of fresh bread to them.
And plunder the rich of their vineyards
with those two blessed hands
which blasted the nails with one blow of light,
and flew away from the Cross!

Eyelash of morning, you cannot lift yourselves!
Give us our daily bread,
Lord . . . !

Every bone in me belongs to others;
and maybe I robbed them.
I came to take something for myself that maybe
was meant for some other man;
and I start thinking that, if I had not been born,
another poor man could have drunk this coffee.
I feel like a dirty thief . . . Where will I end?

And in this frigid hour, when the earth
has the odor of human dust and is so sad,
I wish I could beat on all the doors
and beg pardon from someone,
and make bits of fresh bread for him
here, in the oven of my heart . . . !

THE ETERNAL DICE
(from the Spanish of César Vallejo)

My God, I am weeping for the life that I live;
I am sorry to have stolen your bread;
but this wretched, thinking piece of clay
is not a crust formed in your side:
you have no Marys that abandon you!

My God, if you had been man,
today you would know how to be God;
but you always lived so well,
that now you feel nothing of your own creation.
And the man who suffers you: he is God!

Today, when there are candles in my witchlike eyes,
as in the eyes of a condemned man,
God of mine, you will light all your lamps,
and we will play with the old dice . . .
Gambler, when the whole universe, perhaps,
is thrown down,
the circled eyes of Death will turn up,
like two final aces of clay.

My God, in this muffled, dark night,
you can't play any more, because the Earth
is already a die nicked and rounded
from rolling by chance;
and it can stop only in a hollow place,
in the hollow of the enormous grave.

THE BIG PEOPLE
(from the Spanish of César Vallejo)

What time are the big people
going to come back?
Blind Santiago is striking six
and already it's very dark.

Mother said that she wouldn't be delayed.

Aguedita, Nativa, Miguel,
be careful of going over there, where
doubled-up griefs whimpering their memories
have just gone
toward the quiet poultry yard, where
the hens are still getting settled,
who have been startled so much.
We'd better just stay here.
Mother said that she wouldn't be delayed.

And we shouldn't be sad. Let's go see
the boats — mine is prettier than anybody's! —
we were playing with them the whole blessed day,
without fighting among ourselves, as it should be:
they stayed behind in the puddle, all ready,
loaded with pleasant things for tomorrow.

Let's wait like this, obedient
and helpless, for the homecoming, the apologies
of the big people, who are always the first
to abandon the rest of us in the house —
as if we couldn't get away too!

Aguedita, Nativa, Miguel?
I am calling, I am feeling around for you in the darkness.
Don't leave me behind by myself,
to be locked in all alone.

DOWN TO THE DREGS
(from the Spanish of César Vallejo)

This afternoon it rains as never before; and I
don't feel like staying alive, heart.

The afternoon is pleasant. Why shouldn't it be?
It is wearing grace and pain; it is dressed like a
    woman.

This afternoon in Lima it is raining. And I remember
the cruel caverns of my ingratitude;
my block of ice laid on her poppy,
stronger than her crying "Don't be this way!"

My violent black flowers; and the barbarous
and staggering blow with a stone; and the glacial
    pause.
And the silence of her dignity will pour
scalding oils on the end of the sentence.

Therefore, this afternoon, as never before, I walk
with this owl, with this heart.

And other women go past; and seeing me sullen,
they sip a little of you
in the abrupt furrow of my deep grief.

This afternoon it rains, rains endlessly. And I
don't feel like staying alive, heart.

NOT IN MARBLE PALACES
(from the Spanish of Pedro Salinas)

Not in marble palaces,
not in months, no, nor in ciphers,
never touching ground:
in weightless, fragile worlds
we have lived together.

Time was beaten out,
but hardly by minutes:
one minute was a hundred years,
one life, one love.
Roofs sheltered us,
less than roofs, clouds;
less than clouds, heavens;
even less, air, nothing.
Crossing oceans
formed out of twenty tears,
ten yours and ten mine,
we arrived at the golden
beads of a necklace,
clear islands, deserted,
without flowers, without bodies;
a harbor, so tiny,
made of glass, for a love
that in itself was enough
for the largest longing,
and we asked neither ships
nor time for help.
Opening
enormous tunnels
in grains of sand,
we discovered the mines
of flames and of chance.
And everything
hanging from that thread
that held up . . . what?
That's why our life
doesn't appear to be lived:
slippery, evasive,
it left behind neither wakes
nor footprints. If you want
to remember it, don't look
where you always look for traces
and recollections.
Don't look at your soul,
your shadow or your lips.

Look carefully into the palm
of your hand, it's empty.

ANACREON'S GRAVE
(from the German of Goethe)

Here, where the rose opens,
Where delicate vines and bay leaves embrace each other,
Where the young dove is calling,
Where the little cricket is glad,
Whose grave is this,
That all the gods have planted and trimmed with
    living things?
This is Anacreon's bed.
The happy poet enjoyed spring, summer, and autumn;
Now this small hill shelters him from the winter.

THE BRANCH WILL NOT BREAK

Ach, könnt' ich dorthin kommen,
Und dort mein Herz erfreu'n,
Und aller Qual entnommen,
Und frei und selig sein.

Ach, jenes Land der Wonne!
Das seh' ich oft im Traum.
Doch kommt die Morgensonne,
Zerfliesst's wie eitel Schaum.

ELEUTHERIA

Μνασεσθαι τινα φαιμ υστερου αμμεοιν
(Sappho)

AS I STEP OVER A PUDDLE AT THE END OF WINTER, I THINK OF AN ANCIENT CHINESE GOVERNOR

And how can I, born in evil days
And fresh from failure, ask a kindness
of Fate?
            —Written A.D. 819

Po Chu-i, balding old politician,
What's the use?
I think of you,
Uneasily entering the gorges of the Yang-Tze,
When you were being towed up the rapids
Toward some political job or other
In the city of Chungshou.
You made it, I guess,
By dark.

But it is 1960, it is almost spring again,
And the tall rocks of Minneapolis
Build me my own black twilight
Of bamboo ropes and waters.
Where is Yuan Chen, the friend you loved?
Where is the sea, that once solved the whole loneliness
Of the Midwest? Where is Minneapolis? I can see nothing
But the great terrible oak tree darkening with winter.
Did you find the city of isolated men beyond mountains?
Or have you been holding the end of a frayed rope
For a thousand years?

GOODBYE TO THE POETRY OF CALCIUM

Dark cypresses—
The world is uneasily happy:
It will all be forgotten.
            —THEODOR STORM

Mother of roots, you have not seeded
The tall ashes of loneliness

For me. Therefore,
Now I go.
If I knew the name,
Your name, all trellises of vineyards and old fire
Would quicken to shake terribly my
Earth, mother of spiralling searches, terrible
Fable of calcium, girl. I crept this afternoon
In weeds once more,
Casual, daydreaming you might not strike
Me down. Mother of window sills and journeys,
Hallower of scratching hands,
The sight of my blind man makes me want to weep.
Tiller of waves or whatever, woman or man,
Mother of roots or father of diamonds,
Look: I am nothing.
I do not even have ashes to rub into my eyes.

IN FEAR OF HARVESTS

It has happened
Before: nearby,
The nostrils of slow horses
Breathe evenly,
And the brown bees drag their high garlands,
Heavily,
Toward hives of snow.

THREE STANZAS FROM GOETHE

That man standing there, who is he?
His path lost in the thicket,
Behind him the bushes
Lash back together,
The grass rises again,
The waste devours him.

Oh, who will heal the sufferings
Of the man whose balm turned poison?

Who drank nothing
But hatred of men from love's abundance?
Once despised, now a despiser,
He kills his own life,
The precious secret.
The self-seeker finds nothing.

Oh Father of Love,
If your psaltery holds one tone
That his ear still might echo,
Then quicken his heart!
Open his eyes, shut off by clouds
From the thousand fountains
So near him, dying of thirst
In his own desert.

(NOTE: These three stanzas are from
Goethe's poem "Harzreise im Winter."
They are the stanzas which Brahms
detached from the poem and employed
as the text for his "Alto Rhapsody" of
1869.)

AUTUMN BEGINS IN MARTINS FERRY, OHIO

In the Shreve High football stadium,
I think of Polacks nursing long beers in Tiltonsville,
And gray faces of Negroes in the blast furnace at Benwood,
And the ruptured night watchman of Wheeling Steel,
Dreaming of heroes.

All the proud fathers are ashamed to go home.
Their women cluck like starved pullets,
Dying for love.

Therefore,
Their sons grow suicidally beautiful
At the beginning of October,
And gallop terribly against each other's bodies.

LYING IN A HAMMOCK AT WILLIAM DUFFY'S FARM IN PINE ISLAND, MINNESOTA

Over my head, I see the bronze butterfly,
Asleep on the black trunk,
Blowing like a leaf in green shadow.
Down the ravine behind the empty house,
The cowbells follow one another
Into the distances of the afternoon.
To my right,
In a field of sunlight between two pines,
The droppings of last year's horses
Blaze up into golden stones.
I lean back, as the evening darkens and comes on.
A chicken hawk floats over, looking for home.
I have wasted my life.

THE JEWEL

There is this cave
In the air behind my body
That nobody is going to touch:
A cloister, a silence
Closing around a blossom of fire.
When I stand upright in the wind,
My bones turn to dark emeralds.

IN THE FACE OF HATRED

I am frightened by the sorrow
Of escaping animals.
The snake moves slowly
Beyond his horizon of yellow stone.
A great harvest of convicts has shaken loose
And hurries across the wall of your eyes.
Most of them, all moving alike,
Are gone already along the river.
Only two boys,

114

Trailed by shadows of rooted police,
Turn aimlessly in the lashing elderberries.
One cries for his father's death,
And the other, the silent one,
Listens into the hallway
Of a dark leaf.

FEAR IS WHAT QUICKENS ME

1.
Many animals that our fathers killed in America
Had quick eyes.
They stared about wildly,
When the moon went dark.
The new moon falls into the freight yards
Of cities in the south,
But the loss of the moon to the dark hands of Chicago
Does not matter to the deer
In this northern field.

2.
What is that tall woman doing
There, in the trees?
I can hear rabbits and mourning doves whispering together
In the dark grass, there
Under the trees.

3.
I look about wildly.

A MESSAGE HIDDEN IN AN EMPTY WINE BOTTLE THAT I THREW INTO A GULLY OF MAPLE TREES ONE NIGHT AT AN INDECENT HOUR

Women are dancing around a fire
By a pond of creosote and waste water from the river
In the dank fog of Ohio.
They are dead.

I am alone here,
And I reach for the moon that dangles
Cold on a dark vine.
The unwashed shadows
Of blast furnaces from Moundsville, West Virginia,
Are sneaking across the pits of strip mines
To steal grapes
In heaven.
Nobody else knows I am here.
All right.
Come out, come out, I am dying.
I am growing old.
An owl rises
From the cutter bar
Of a hayrake.

STAGES ON A JOURNEY WESTWARD

1.
I began in Ohio.
I still dream of home.
Near Mansfield, enormous dobbins enter dark barns in autumn,
Where they can be lazy, where they can munch little apples,
Or sleep long.
But by night now, in the bread lines my father
Prowls, I cannot find him: So far off,
1500 miles or so away, and yet
I can hardy sleep.
In a blue rag the old man limps to my bed,
Leading a blind horse
Of gentleness.
In 1932, grimy with machinery, he sang me
A lullaby of a goosegirl.
Outside the house, the slag heaps waited.

2.
In western Minnesota, just now,
I slept again.
In my dream, I crouched over a fire.

The only human beings between me and the Pacific Ocean
Were old Indians, who wanted to kill me.
They squat and stare for hours into small fires
Far off in the mountains.
The blades of their hatchets are dirty with the grease
Of huge, silent buffaloes.

3.
It is dawn.
I am shivering,
Even beneath a huge eiderdown.
I came in last night, drunk,
And left the oil stove cold.
I listen a long time, now, to the flurries.
Snow howls all around me, out of the abandoned prairies.
It sounds like the voices of bums and gamblers,
Rattling through the bare nineteenth-century whorehouses
In Nevada.

4.
Defeated for re-election,
The half-educated sheriff of Mukilteo, Washington,
Has been drinking again.
He leads me up the cliff, tottering.
Both drunk, we stand among the graves.
Miners paused here on the way up to Alaska.
Angry, they spaded their broken women's bodies
Into ditches of crab grass.
I lie down between tombstones.
At the bottom of the cliff
America is over and done with.
America,
Plunged into the dark furrows
Of the sea again.

HOW MY FEVER LEFT

I can still hear her.
She hobbles downstairs to the kitchen.

She is swearing at the dishes.
She slaps her grease rags
Into a basket,
And slings it over her skinny forearm, crooked
With hatred, and stomps outside.
I can hear my father downstairs,
Standing without a coat in the open back door,
Calling to the old bat across the snow.
She's forgotten her black shawl,
But I see her through my window, sneering,
Flapping upward
Toward some dark church on the hill.
She has to meet somebody else, and
It's no use, she won't listen,
She's gone.

MINERS

1.

The police are probing tonight for the bodies
Of children in the black waters
Of the suburbs.

2.

Below the chemical riffles of the Ohio River,
Grappling hooks
Drag delicately about, between skiff hulks and sand shoals,
Until they clasp
Fingers.

3.

Somewhere in a vein of Bridgeport, Ohio;
Deep in a coal hill behind Hanna's name;
Below the tipples, and dark as a drowsy woodchuck;
A man, alone,
Stumbles upon the outside locks of a grave, whispering
Oh let me in.

4.
Many American women mount long stairs
In the shafts of houses,
Fall asleep, and emerge suddenly into tottering palaces.

IN OHIO

White mares lashed to the sulky carriages
Trot softly
Around the dismantled fairgrounds
Near Buckeye Lake.

The sandstone blocks of a wellspring
Cool dark green moss.

The sun floats down, a small golden lemon dissolves
In the water.
I dream, as I lean over the edge, of a crawdad's mouth.

The cellars of haunted houses are like ancient cities,
Fallen behind a big heap of apples.

A widow on a front porch puckers her lips
And whispers.

TWO POEMS ABOUT PRESIDENT HARDING

ONE: *His Death*
In Marion, the honey locust trees are falling.
Everybody in town remembers the white hair,
The campaign of a lost summer, the front porch
Open to the public, and the vaguely stunned smile
Of a lucky man.

"Neighbor, I want to be helpful," he said once.
Later, "You think I'm honest, don't you?"
Weeping drunk.

I am drunk this evening in 1961,
In a jag for my countryman,
Who died of crab meat on the way back from Alaska.
Everyone knows that joke.

How many honey locusts have fallen,
Pitched rootlong into the open graves of strip mines,
Since the First World War ended
And Wilson the gaunt deacon jogged sullenly
Into silence?
Tonight,
The cancerous ghosts of old con men
Shed their leaves.
For a proud man,
Lost between the turnpike near Cleveland
And the chiropractors' signs looming among dead mul-
      berry trees,
There is no place left to go
But home.

"Warren lacks mentality," one of his friends said.

Yet he was beautiful, he was the snowfall
Turned to white stallions standing still
Under dark elm trees.

He died in public. He claimed the secret right
To be ashamed.

Two: *His Tomb in Ohio*

"...he died of a busted gut."
      — MENCKEN, on BRYAN.

A hundred slag piles north of us,
At the mercy of the moon and rain,
He lies in his ridiculous
Tomb, our fellow citizen.
No, I have never seen that place,

Where many shadows of faceless thieves
Chuckle and stumble and embrace
On beer cans, stogie butts, and graves.

One holiday, one rainy week
After the country fell apart,
Hoover and Coolidge came to speak
And snivel about his broken heart.
His grave, a huge absurdity,
Embarrassed cops and visitors.
Hoover and Coolidge crept away
By night, and women closed their doors.

Now junkmen call their children in
Before they catch their death of cold;
Young lovers let the moon begin
Its quick spring; and the day grows old;
The mean one-legger who rakes up leaves
Has chased the loafers out of the park;
Minnegan Leonard half-believes
In God, and the poolroom goes dark;

America goes on, goes on
Laughing, and Harding was a fool.
Even his big pretentious stone
Lays him bare to ridicule.
I know it. But don't look at me.
By God, I didn't start this mess.
Whatever moon and rain may be,
The hearts of men are merciless.

EISENHOWER'S VISIT TO FRANCO, 1959

" . . . we die of cold, and not of darkness."
     — UNAMUNO

The American hero must triumph over
The forces of darkness.
He has flown through the very light of heaven

And come down in the slow dusk
Of Spain.

Franco stands in a shining circle of police.
His arms open in welcome.
He promises all dark things
Will be hunted down.

State police yawn in the prisons.
Antonio Machado follows the moon
Down a road of white dust,
To a cave of silent children
Under the Pyrenees.
Wine darkens in stone jars in villages.
Wine sleeps in the mouths of old men, it is a dark red color.

Smiles glitter in Madrid.
Eisenhower has touched hands with Franco, embracing
In a glare of photographers.
Clean new bombers from America muffle their engines
And glide down now.
Their wings shine in the searchlights
Of bare fields,
In Spain.

IN MEMORY OF A SPANISH POET

Take leave of the sun, and of the wheat, for me.
            — MIGUEL HERNÁNDEZ,
            written in prison, 1942.

I see you strangling
Under the black ripples of whitewashed walls.
Your hands turn yellow in the ruins of the sun.
I dream of your slow voice, flying,
Planting the dark waters of the spirit
With lutes and seeds.

Here, in the American Midwest,
Those seeds fly out of the field and across the strange heaven of my skull.
They scatter out of their wings a quiet farewell,
A greeting to my country.

Now twilight gathers,
A long sundown.
Silos creep away toward the west.

THE UNDERMINING OF THE DEFENSE ECONOMY

Stairway, face, window,
Mottled animals
Running over the public buildings.
Maple and elm.
In the autumn
Of early evening,
A pumpkin
Lies on its side,
Turning yellow as the face
Of a discharged general.
It's no use complaining, the economy
Is going to hell with all these radical
Changes,
Girls the color of butterflies
That can't be sold.
Only after nightfall,
Little boys lie still, awake,
Wondering, wondering,
Delicate little boxes of dust.

TWILIGHTS

The big stones of the cistern behind the barn
Are soaked in whitewash.
My grandmother's face is a small maple leaf
Pressed in a secret box.
Locusts are climbing down into the dark green crevices
Of my childhood. Latches click softly in the trees. Your hair is gray.

The arbors of the cities are withered.
Far off, the shopping centers empty and darken.

A red shadow of steel mills.

TWO HANGOVERS

NUMBER ONE
I slouch in bed.
Beyond the streaked trees of my window,
All groves are bare.
Locusts and poplars change to unmarried women
Sorting slate from anthracite
Between railroad ties:
The yellow-bearded winter of the depression
Is still alive somewhere, an old man
Counting his collection of bottle caps
In a tarpaper shack under the cold trees
Of my grave.

I still feel half drunk,
And all those old women beyond my window
Are hunching toward the graveyard.

Drunk, mumbling Hungarian,
The sun staggers in,
And his big stupid face pitches
Into the stove.
For two hours I have been dreaming
Of green butterflies searching for diamonds

124

In coal seams;
And children chasing each other for a game
Through the hills of fresh graves.
But the sun has come home drunk from the sea,
And a sparrow outside
Sings of the Hanna Coal Co. and the dead moon.
The filaments of cold light bulbs tremble
In music like delicate birds.
Ah, turn it off.

NUMBER TWO: I TRY TO WAKEN AND GREET THE WORLD ONCE AGAIN
In a pine tree,
A few yards away from my window sill,
A brilliant blue jay is springing up and down, up and
      down,
On a branch.
I laugh, as I see him abandon himself
To entire delight, for he knows as well as I do
That the branch will not break.

DEPRESSED BY A BOOK OF BAD POETRY, I WALK TOWARD AN UNUSED PASTURE AND INVITE THE INSECTS TO JOIN ME

Relieved, I let the book fall behind a stone.
I climb a slight rise of grass.
I do not want to disturb the ants
Who are walking single file up the fence post,
Carrying small white petals,
Casting shadows so frail that I can see through them.
I close my eyes for a moment, and listen.
The old grasshoppers
Are tired, they leap heavily now,
Their thighs are burdened.
I want to hear them, they have clear sounds to make.
Then lovely, far off, a dark cricket begins
In the maple trees.

TWO HORSES PLAYING IN THE ORCHARD

Too soon, too soon, a man will come
To lock the gate, and drive them home.
Then, neighing softly through the night,
The mare will nurse her shoulder bite.
Now, lightly fair, through lock and mane
She gazes over the dusk again,
And sees her darkening stallion leap
In grass for apples, half asleep.

Lightly, lightly, on slender knees
He turns, lost in a dream of trees.
Apples are slow to find this day,
Someone has stolen the best away.
Still, some remain before the snow,
A few, trembling on boughs so low
A horse can reach them, small and sweet:
And some are tumbling to her feet.

Too soon, a man will scatter them,
Although I do not know his name,
His age, or how he came to own
A horse, an apple tree, a stone.
I let those horses in to steal
On principle, because I feel
Like half a horse myself, although
Too soon, too soon, already. Now.

BY A LAKE IN MINNESOTA

Upshore from the cloud —
The slow whale of country twilight —
The spume of light falls into valleys
Full of roses.

And below,
Out of the placid waters,
Two beavers, mother and child,

126

Wave out long ripples
To the dust of dead leaves
On the shore.

And the moon walks,
Hunting for hidden dolphins
Behind the darkening combers
Of the ground.

And downshore from the cloud,
I stand, waiting
For dark.

BEGINNING

The moon drops one or two feathers into the field.
The dark wheat listens.
Be still.
Now.
There they are, the moon's young, trying
Their wings.
Between trees, a slender woman lifts up the lovely shadow
Of her face, and now she steps into the air, now she is gone
Wholly, into the air.
I stand alone by an elder tree, I do not dare breathe
Or move.
I listen.
The wheat leans back toward its own darkness,
And I lean toward mine.

FROM A BUS WINDOW IN CENTRAL OHIO,
JUST BEFORE A THUNDER SHOWER

Cribs loaded with roughage huddle together
Before the north clouds.
The wind tiptoes between poplars.
The silver maple leaves squint
Toward the ground.

An old farmer, his scarlet face
Apologetic with whiskey, swings back a barn door
And calls a hundred black-and-white Holsteins
From the clover field.

MARCH

A bear under the snow
Turns over to yawn.
It's been a long, hard rest.

Once, as she lay asleep, her cubs fell
Out of her hair,
And she did not know them.

It is hard to breathe
In a tight grave:

So she roars,
And the roof breaks.
Dark rivers and leaves
Pour down.

When the wind opens its doors
In its own good time,
The cubs follow that relaxed and beautiful
        woman
Outside to the unfamiliar cities
Of moss.

TRYING TO PRAY

This time, I have left my body behind me, crying
In its dark thorns.
Still,
There are good things in this world.
It is dusk.
It is the good darkness

Of women's hands that touch loaves.
The spirit of a tree begins to move.
I touch leaves.
I close my eyes, and think of water.

TWO SPRING CHARMS

fragments from the Norwegian
1.
Now it is late winter.

Years ago,
I walked through a spring wind
Bending green wheat
In a field near Trondhjem.

2.
Black snow,
Like a strange sea creature,
Draws back into itself,
Restoring grass to earth.

SPRING IMAGES

Two athletes
Are dancing in the cathedral
Of the wind.

A butterfly lights on the branch
Of your green voice.

Small antelopes
Fall asleep in the ashes
Of the moon.

ARRIVING IN THE COUNTRY AGAIN

The white house is silent.
My friends can't hear me yet.
The flicker who lives in the bare tree at the
    field's edge
Pecks once and is still for a long time.
I stand still in the late afternoon.
My face is turned away from the sun.
A horse grazes in my long shadow.

IN THE COLD HOUSE

I slept a few minutes ago,
Even though the stove has been out for hours.
I am growing old.
A bird cries in bare elder trees.

SNOWSTORM IN THE MIDWEST

Though haunches of whales
Slope into whitecap doves,
It is hard to drown here.

Between two walls,
A fold of echoes,
A girl's voice walks naked.

I step into the water
Of two flakes.
The crowns of white birds rise
To my ankles,
To my knees,
To my face.

Escaping in silence
From locomotive and smoke,
I hunt the huge feathers of gulls

And the fountains of hills,
I hunt the sea, to walk on the waters.

A splayed starling
Follows me down a long stairway
Of white sand.

HAVING LOST MY SONS, I CONFRONT THE WRECKAGE OF THE MOON: CHRISTMAS, 1960

After dark
Near the South Dakota border,
The moon is out hunting, everywhere,
Delivering fire,
And walking down hallways
Of a diamond.

Behind a tree,
It lights on the ruins
Of a white city:
Frost, frost.

Where are they gone,
Who lived there?

Bundled away under wings
And dark faces.

I am sick
Of it, and I go on,
Living, alone, alone,
Past the charred silos, past the hidden graves
Of Chippewas and Norwegians.

This cold winter
Moon spills the inhuman fire
Of jewels
Into my hands.

Dead riches, dead hands, the moon
Darkens,
And I am lost in the beautiful white ruins
Of America.

AMERICAN WEDDING

She dreamed long of waters.
Inland today, she wakens
On scraped knees, lost
Among locust thorns.

She gropes for
The path backward, to
The pillows of the sea.

Bruised trillium
Of wilderness, she
May rest on briar leaves,
As long as the wind cares to pause.

Now she is going to learn
How it is that animals
Can save time:
They sleep a whole season
Of lamentation and snow,
Without bothering to weep.

A PRAYER TO ESCAPE FROM THE MARKET PLACE

I renounce the blindness of the magazines.
I want to lie down under a tree.
This is the only duty that is not death.
This is the everlasting happiness
Of small winds.
Suddenly,
A pheasant flutters, and I turn

Only to see him vanishing at the damp edge
Of the road.

RAIN

It is the sinking of things.

Flashlights drift over dark trees,
Girls kneel,
An owl's eyelids fall.

The sad bones of my hands descend into a valley
Of strange rocks.

TODAY I WAS HAPPY, SO I MADE THIS POEM

As the plump squirrel scampers
Across the roof of the corncrib,
The moon suddenly stands up in the darkness,
And I see that it is impossible to die.
Each moment of time is a mountain.
An eagle rejoices in the oak trees of heaven,
Crying
This is what I wanted.

MARY BLY

I sit here, doing nothing, alone, worn out by long winter.
I feel the light breath of the newborn child.
Her face is smooth as the side of an apricot,
Eyes quick as her blond mother's hands.
She has full, soft, red hair, and as she lies quiet
In her tall mother's arms, her delicate hands
Weave back and forth.
I feel the seasons changing beneath me,
Under the floor.
She is braiding the waters of air into the plaited manes

Of happy colts.
They canter, without making a sound, along the shores
Of melting snow.

TO THE EVENING STAR: CENTRAL MINNESOTA

Under the water tower at the edge of town
A hugh Airedale ponders a long ripple
In the grass fields beyond.
Miles off, a whole grove silently
Flies up into the darkness.
One light comes on in the sky,
One lamp on the prairie.

Beautiful daylight of the body, your hands carry seashells.
West of this wide plain,
Animals wilder than ours
Come down from the green mountains in the darkness.
Now they can see you, they know
The open meadows are safe.

I WAS AFRAID OF DYING

Once,
I was afraid of dying
In a field of dry weeds.
But now,
All day long I have been walking among damp fields,
Trying to keep still, listening
To insects that move patiently.
Perhaps they are sampling the fresh dew that gathers slowly
In empty snail shells
And in the secret shelters of sparrow feathers fallen on the
    earth.

A BLESSING

Just off the highway to Rochester, Minnesota,
Twilight bounds softly forth on the grass.
And the eyes of those two Indian ponies
Darken with kindness.
They have come gladly out of the willows
To welcome my friend and me.
We step over the barbed wire into the pasture
Where they have been grazing all day, alone.
They ripple tensely, they can hardly contain their
    happiness
That we have come.
They bow shyly as wet swans. They love each other.
There is no loneliness like theirs.
At home once more,
They begin munching the young tufts of spring in the
    darkness.
I would like to hold the slenderer one in my arms,
For she has walked over to me
And nuzzled my left hand.
She is black and white,
Her mane falls wild on her forehead,
And the light breeze moves me to caress her long ear
That is delicate as the skin over a girl's wrist.
Suddenly I realize
That if I stepped out of my body I would break
Into blossom.

MILKWEED

While I stood here, in the open, lost in myself,
I must have looked a long time
Down the corn rows, beyond grass,
The small house,
White walls, animals lumbering toward the barn.
I look down now. It is all changed.
Whatever it was I lost, whatever I wept for
Was a wild, gentle thing, the small dark eyes

Loving me in secret.
It is here. At a touch of my hand,
The air fills with delicate creatures
From the other world.

A DREAM OF BURIAL

Nothing was left of me
But my right foot
And my left shoulder.
They lay white as the skein of a spider floating
In a field of snow toward a dark building
Tilted and stained by wind.
Inside the dream, I dreamed on.

A parade of old women
Sang softly above me,
Faint mosquitoes near still water.

So I waited, in my corridor.
I listened for the sea
To call me.
I knew that, somewhere outside, the horse
Stood saddled, browsing in grass,
Waiting for me.

SHALL WE GATHER AT THE RIVER

Und wenn der Mensch in seiner Qual verstummt,
Gab mir ein Gott zu sagen, was ich leide.

(Goethe)

Jenny

A CHRISTMAS GREETING

Good evening, Charlie. Yes, I know. You rise,
Two lean gray spiders drifting through your eyes.
Poor Charlie, hobbling down the hill to find
The last bootlegger who might strike them blind,
Be dead. A child, I saw you hunch your spine,
Wrench your left elbow round, to hold in line
The left-hand hollow of your back, as though
The kidney prayed for mercy. Years ago.
The kidneys do not pray, the kidneys drip.
Urine stains at the liver; lip by lip,
Affectionate, the snub-nosed demons kiss
And sting us back to such a world as this.
Charlie, the moon drips slowly in the dark,
The mill smoke stains the snow, the gray whores walk,
The left-hand hollow fills up, like the tide
Drowning the moon, skillful with suicide.
Charlie, don't ask me. Charlie go away,
I feel my own spine hunching. If I pray,
I lose all meaning. I don't know my kind:
Sack me, or bury me among the blind.
What should I pray for? what can they forgive?
You died because you could not bear to live,
Pitched off the bridge in Brookside, God knows why.
Well, don't remind me. I'm afraid to die,
It hurts to die, although the lucky do.
Charlie, I don't know what to say to you
Except Good Evening, Greetings, and Good Night,
God Bless Us Every One. Your grave is white.
What are you doing here?

THE MINNEAPOLIS POEM

to John Logan

I.
I wonder how many old men last winter
Hungry and frightened by namelessness prowled

The Mississippi shore
Lashed blind by the wind, dreaming
Of suicide in the river.
The police remove their cadavers by daybreak
And turn them in somewhere.
Where?
How does the city keep lists of its fathers
Who have no names?
By Nicollet Island I gaze down at the dark water
So beautifully slow.
And I wish my brothers good luck
And a warm grave.

2.
The Chippewa young men
Stab one another shrieking
Jesus Christ.
Split-lipped homosexuals limp in terror of assault.
High school backfields search under benches
Near the Post Office. Their faces are the rich
Raw bacon without eyes.
The Walker Art Center crowd stare
At the Guthrie Theater.

3.
Tall Negro girls from Chicago
Listen to light songs.
They know when the supposed patron
Is a plainclothesman.
A cop's palm
Is a roach dangling down the scorched fangs
Of a light bulb.
The soul of a cop's eyes
Is an eternity of Sunday daybreak in the suburbs
Of Juárez, Mexico.

4.
The legless beggars are gone, carried away
By white birds.
The Artificial Limbs Exchange is gutted

140

And sown with lime.
The whalebone crutches and hand-me-down trusses
Huddle together dreaming in a desolation
Of dry groins.
I think of poor men astonished to waken
Exposed in broad daylight by the blade
Of a strange plough.

5.
All over the walls of comb cells
Automobiles perfumed and blindered
Consent with a mutter of high good humor
To take their two naps a day.
Without sound windows glide back
Into dusk.
The sockets of a thousand blind bee graves tier upon tier
Tower not quite toppling.
There are men in this city who labor dawn after dawn
To sell me my death.

6.
But I could not bear
To allow my poor brother my body to die
In Minneapolis.
The old man Walt Whitman our countryman
Is now in America our country
Dead.
But he was not buried in Minneapolis
At least.
And no more may I be
Please God.

7.
I want to be lifted up
By some great white bird unknown to the police,
And soar for a thousand miles and be carefully hidden
Modest and golden as one last corn grain,
Stored with the secrets of the wheat and the mysterious lives
Of the unnamed poor.

INSCRIPTION FOR THE TANK

My life was never so precious
To me as now.
I gape unbelieving at those two lines
Of my words, caught and frisked naked.

If they loomed secret and dim
On the wall of the drunk-tank,
Scraped there by a raw fingernail
In the trickling crusts of gray mold,

Surely the plainest thug who read them
Would cluck with the ancient pity.
Men have a right to thank God for their loneliness.
The walls are hysterical with their dank messages.

But the last hophead is gone
With the quick of his name
Bleeding away down a new wall
Blank as his nails.

I wish I had walked outside
To wade in the sea, drowsing and soothed;
I wish I had copied some words from Isaiah,
Kabir, Ansari, oh Whitman, oh anyone, anyone.

But I wrote down mine, and now
I must read them forever, even
When the wings in my shoulders cringe up
At the cold's fangs, as now.

Of all my lives, the one most secret to me,
Folded deep in a book never written,
Locked up in a dream of a still place,
I have blurted out.

I have heard weeping in secret
And quick nails broken.

Let the dead pray for their own dead.
What is their pity to me?

IN TERROR OF HOSPITAL BILLS

I still have some money
To eat with, alone
And frightened, knowing how soon
I will waken a poor man.

It snows freely and freely hardens
On the lawns of my hope, my secret
Hounded and flayed. I wonder
What words to beg money with.

Pardon me, sir, could you?
Which way is St. Paul?
I thirst.
I am a full-blooded Sioux Indian.

Soon I am sure to become so hungry
I will have to leap barefoot through gas-fire veils of shame,
I will have to stalk timid strangers
On the whorehouse corners.

Oh moon, sow leaves on my hands,
On my seared face, oh I love you.
My throat is open, insane,
Tempting pneumonia.

But my life was never so precious
To me as now.
I will have to beg coins
After dark.

I will learn to scent the police,
And sit or go blind, stay mute, be taken for dead
For your sake, oh my secret,
My life.

I AM A SIOUX BRAVE, HE SAID IN MINNEAPOLIS

1.

He is just plain drunk.
He knows no more than I do
What true waters to mourn for
Or what kind of words to sing
When he dies.

2.

The black caterpillar
Crawls out, what with one thing
And another, across
The wet road.
How lonely the dead must be.

GAMBLING IN STATELINE, NEVADA

The great cracked shadow of the Sierra Nevada
Hoods over the last road.

I came down here from the side of
A cold cairn where a girl named Rachel
Just made it inside California
And died of bad luck.

Here, across from the keno board,
An old woman
Has been beating a strange machine
In its face all day.

Dusk limps past in the street.
I step outside.
It's gone.
I finger a worthless agate
In my pocket.

THE POOR WASHED UP BY CHICAGO WINTER

Well, I still have a train ticket valid.
I can get out.
The faces of unimaginably beautiful blind men
Glide among mountains.
What pinnacles should they gaze upon
Except the moon?
Eight miles down in the secret canyons and ranges
Of six o'clock, the poor
Are mountainously blind and invisible.
Do they die?
Where are they buried?
They fill the sea now.
When you glide in, men cast shadows
You can trace from an airplane.
Their shoulders are huge with the barnacles
That God has cast down into the deep places.
The Sixth Day remained evening, deepening further down,
Further and further down, into night, a wounded black angel
Forgotten by Genesis.
If only the undulating of the shadows would pause.
The sea can stand anything.
I can't.

I can remember the evening.
I can remember the morning.
I am too young
To live in the sea alone without
Any company.
I can either move into the McCormick Theological Seminary
And get a night's sleep,
Or else get hauled back to Minneapolis.

AN ELEGY FOR THE POET MORGAN BLUM

Morgan the lonely,
Morgan the dead,
Has followed his only

Child into a vast
Desolatiòn.
When I heard he was going
I tried to blossom
Into the boat beside him,
But I had no money.

When I went in to see him,
The nurse said no.
So I snuck in behind her.
And there they were.
They were there, for a moment.
Red Jacket, Robert Hayman,
H. Phelps Putnam,
And sweet Ted Roethke,
A canary and a bear.

They looked me over,
More or less alive.
They looked at me, more
Or less out of place.
They said, get out,
Morgan is dying.
They said, get out,
Leave him alone.

We have no kings
In this country,
They kept saying.
But we have one
Where the dead rise
On the other shore.
And they hear only
The cold owls throwing
Salt over
Their secret shoulders.

So I left Morgan,
And all of them alone.
And now I am so lonely

For the air I want to breathe.
Come breathe me, dark prince.
And Morgan lay there
Clean shaved like a baby
By the nurse who said no.
And so a couple
Of years ago,
The old poets died
Young.

And now the young,
Scarlet on their wings, fly away
Over the marshes.

OLD AGE COMPENSATION

There are no roads but the frost,
And the pumpkins look haggard.
The ants have gone down to the grave, crying
God spare them one green blade.
Failing the grass, they have abandoned the grass.
All creatures who have died today of old age
Have gone more than ten miles already.
All day I have slogged behind
And dreamed of them praying for one candle,
Only one.
Fair enough. Only, from where I stand,
I can see one last night nurse shining in one last window
In the Home for Senior Citizens.
The white uniform flickers, the town is gone.
What do I do now? I have one candle,
But what's the use?
If only they can catch up with twilight,
They'll be safe enough.
Their boats are moored there, among the cattails
And the night-herons' nests.
All they have to do now
Is to get one of those lazy birds awake long enough
To guide them across the river.

Herons fly low, too.
All it will take is one old man trawling one oar.
Anybody can follow a blue wing,
They don't need my candle.
But I do.

BEFORE A CASHIER'S WINDOW IN A DEPARTMENT STORE

1.
The beautiful cashier's white face has risen once more
Behind a young manager's shoulder.
They whisper together, and stare
Straight into my face.
I feel like grabbing a stray child
Or a skinny old woman
And driving into a cellar, crouching
Under a stone bridge, praying myself sick,
Till the troops pass.

2.
Why should he care? He goes.
I slump deeper.
In my frayed coat, I am pinned down
By debt. He nods,
Commending my flesh to the pity of the daws of God.

3.
Am I dead? And, if not, why not?
For she sails there, alone, looming in the
        heaven of the beautiful.
She knows
The bulldozers will scrape me up
After dark, behind
The officers' club.
Beneath her terrible blaze, my skeleton
Glitters out. I am the dark. I am the dark
Bone I was born to be.

4.
Tu Fu woke shuddering on a battlefield
Once, in the dead of night, and made out
The mangled women, sorting
The haggard slant-eyes.
The moon was up.

5.
I am hungry. In two more days
It will be spring. So this
Is what it feels like.

SPEAK

To speak in a flat voice
Is all that I can do.
I have gone every place
Asking for you.
Wondering where to turn
And how the search would end
And the last streetlight spin
Above me blind.

Then I returned rebuffed
And saw under the sun
The race not to the swift
Nor the battle won.
Liston dives in the tank,
Lord, in Lewiston, Maine,
And Ernie Doty's drunk
In hell again.

And Jenny, oh my Jenny
Whom I love, rhyme be damned,
Has broken her spare beauty
In a whorehouse old.
She left her new baby
In a bus-station can,

And sprightly danced away
Through Jacksontown.

Which is a place I know,
One where I got picked up
A few shrunk years ago
By a good cop.
Believe it, Lord, or not.
Don't ask me who he was.
I speak of flat defeat
In a flat voice.

I have gone forward with
Some, a few lonely some.
They have fallen to death.
I die with them.
Lord, I have loved Thy cursed,
The beauty of Thy house:
Come down. Come down. Why dost
Thou hide thy face?

OUTSIDE FARGO, NORTH DAKOTA

Along the sprawled body of the derailed
    Great Northern freight car,
I strike a match slowly and lift it slowly.
No wind.

Beyond town, three heavy white horses
Wade all the way to their shoulders
In a silo shadow.

Suddenly the freight car lurches.
The door slams back, a man with a flashlight
Calls me good evening.
I nod as I write good evening, lonely
And sick for home.

LIVING BY THE RED RIVER

Blood flows in me, but what does it have to do
With the rain that is falling?
In me, scarlet-jacketed armies march into the rain
Across dark fields. My blood lies still,
Indifferent to cannons on the ships of imperialists
Drifting offshore.
Sometimes I have to sleep
In dangerous places, on cliffs underground,
Walls that still hold the whole prints
Of ancient ferns.

TO FLOOD STAGE AGAIN

In Fargo, North Dakota, a man
Warned me the river might rise
To flood stage again.
On the bridge, a girl hurries past me, alone,
Unhappy face.
Will she pause in wet grass somewhere?
Behind my eyes she stands tiptoe, yearning
      for confused sparrows
To fetch a bit of string and dried wheatbeard
To line her outstretched hand.
I open my eyes and gaze down
At the dark water.

A POEM WRITTEN UNDER AN ARCHWAY IN A DISCONTINUED RAILROAD STATION, FARGO, NORTH DAKOTA

Outside the great clanging cathedrals of rust and smoke,
The locomotives browse on sidings.
They pause, exhausted by the silence of prairies.
Sometimes they leap and cry out, skitterish.
They fear dark little boys in Ohio,
Who know how to giggle without breathing,

Who sneak out of graveyards in summer twilights
And lay crossties across rails.
The rattle of coupling pins still echoes
In the smoke stains,
The Cincinnati of the dead.
Around the bend now, beyond the grain elevators,
The late afternoon limited wails
Savage with the horror and loneliness of a child, lost
And dragged by a glad cop through a Chicago terminal.
The noose tightens, the wail stops, and I am leaving.
Across the street, an arthritic man
Takes coins at the parking lot.
He smiles with the sinister grief
Of old age.

LATE NOVEMBER IN A FIELD

Today I am walking alone in a bare place,
And winter is here.
Two squirrels near a fence post
Are helping each other drag a branch
Toward a hiding place; it must be somewhere
Behind those ash trees.
They are still alive, they ought to save acorns
Against the cold.
Frail paws rifle the troughs between cornstalks
        when the moon
Is looking away.
The earth is hard now,
The soles of my shoes need repairs.
I have nothing to ask a blessing for,
Except these words.
I wish they were
Grass.

THE FRONTIER

The man on the radio mourns
That another endless American winter
Daybreak is beginning to fall
On Idaho, on the mountains.

How many scrawny children
Lie dead and half-hidden among frozen ruts
In my body, along my dark roads.
Lean coyotes pass among clouds
On mountain trails, and smile,
And pass on in snow.

A girl stands in a doorway.
Her arms are bare to the elbows,
Her face gray, she stares coldly
At the daybreak.
When the howl goes up, her eyes
Flare white, like a mare's.

LISTENING TO THE MOURNERS

Crouched down by a roadside windbreak
At the edge of the prairie,
I flinch under the baleful jangling of wind
Through the telephone wires, a wilderness of voices
Blown for a thousand miles, for a hundred years.
They all have the same name, and the name is lost.
So: it is not me, it is not my love
Alone lost.
The grief that I hear is my life somewhere.
Now I am speaking with the voice
Of a scarecrow that stands up
And suddenly turns into a bird.
This field is the beginning of my native land,
This place of skull where I hear myself weeping.

YOUTH

Strange bird,
His song remains secret.
He worked too hard to read books.
He never heard how Sherwood Anderson
Got out of it, and fled to Chicago, furious to free himself
From his hatred of factories.
My father toiled fifty years
At Hazel-Atlas Glass,
Caught among girders that smash the kneecaps
Of dumb honyaks.
Did he shudder with hatred in the cold shadow of grease?
Maybe. But my brother and I do know
He came home as quiet as the evening.

He will be getting dark, soon,
And loom through new snow.
I know his ghost will drift home
To the Ohio River, and sit down, alone,
Whittling a root.
He will say nothing.
The waters flow past, older, younger
Than he is, or I am.

RIP

It can't be the passing of time that casts
That white shadow across the waters
Just offshore.
I shiver a little, with the evening.
I turn down the steep path to find
What's left of the river gold.
I whistle a dog lazily, and lazily
A bird whistles me.
Close by a big river, I am alive in my own country,
I am home again.
Yes: I lived here, and here, and my name,
That I carved young, with a girl's, is healed over, now,

And lies sleeping beneath the inward sky
Of a tree's skin, close to the quick.
It's best to keep still.
But:
There goes that bird that whistled me down here
To the river a moment ago.
Who is he? A little white barn owl from Hudson's Bay,
Flown out of his range here, and lost?
Oh, let him be home here, and, if he wants to,
He can be the body that casts
That white shadow across the waters
Just offshore.

THE LIFE

Murdered, I went, risen,
Where the murderers are,
That black ditch
Of river.

And if I come back to my only country
With a white rose on my shoulder,
What is that to you?
It is the grave
In blossom.

It is the trillium of darkness,
It is hell, it is the beginning of winter,
It is a ghost town of Etruscans who have no names
Any more.

It is the old loneliness.
It is.
And it is
The last time.

THREE SENTENCES FOR A DEAD SWAN

1.

There they are now,
The wings,
And I heard them beginning to starve
Between two cold white shadows,
But I dreamed they would rise
Together,
My black Ohioan swan.

2.

Now one after another I let the black scales fall
From the beautiful black spine
Of this lonesome dragon that is born on the earth at last,
My black fire,
Ovoid of my darkness,
Machine-gunned and shattered hillsides of yellow trees
In the autumn of my blood where the apples
Purse their wild lips and smirk knowingly
That my love is dead.

3.

Here, carry his splintered bones
Slowly, slowly
Back into the
Tar and chemical strangled tomb,
The strange water, the
Ohio river, that is no tomb to
Rise from the dead
From.

BRUSH FIRE

In this field,
Where the small animals ran from a brush fire,
It is a voice
In burned weeds, saying
I love you.

Still, when I go there,
I find only two gray stones,
And, lying between them,
A dead bird the color of slate.
It lies askew in its wings,
Its throat bent back as if at the height
    of some joy too great
To bear to give.

And the lights are going out
In a farmhouse, evening
Stands, in a gray frock, silent, at the far side
Of a raccoon's grave.

THE LIGHTS IN THE HALLWAY

The lights in the hallway
Have been out a long time.
I clasp her,
Terrified by the roundness of the earth
And its apples and the voluptuous rings
Of poplar trees, the secret Africas,
The children they give us.
She is slim enough.
Her knee feels like the face
Of a surprised lioness
Nursing the lost children
Of a gazelle by pure accident.
In that body I long for,
The Gabon poets gaze for hours
Between boughs toward heaven, their noble faces
Too secret to weep.
How do I know what color her hair is? I float among
Lonely animals, longing
For the red spider who is God.

THE SMALL BLUE HERON

1.

He is not the last one.
I wish he were. Do I?
My friends brought him into the kitchen
In a waste basket and
Took him out and
Set him down.
I stroked his long throat
On the floor. I was glad to hear him
Croaking with terror.

2.

The Nazis assigned
A dour man
To drive a truck every morning.
They called him "King of the Jews."
One evening, a dour man,
An Old Jew, sought out the King.
"You! Schmo! When you pick me up tomorrow,
Put me on top of the stack,
I've got asthma."

3.

He is not the last one. There is a darkening place
Among the cattails on the other side of the river.
The blue heron has gone there this evening,
Darkening into a reed that the fastidious fox
Never dreamed of.

WILLY LYONS

My uncle, a craftsman of hammers and wood,
Is dead in Ohio.
And my mother cries she is angry.
Willy was buried with nothing except a jacket
Stitched on his shoulder bones.
It is nothing to mourn for.

158

It is the other world.
She does not know how the roan horses, there,
Dead for a century,
Plod slowly.
Maybe they believe Willy's brown coffin, tangled heavily
    in moss,
Is a horse trough drifted to shore
Along that river under the willows and grass.
Let my mother weep on, she needs to, she knows of cold winds.
The long box is empty.
The horses turn back toward the river.
Willy planes limber trees by the waters,
Fitting his boat together.
We may as well let him go.
Nothing is left of Willy on this side
But one cracked ball-peen hammer and one suit,
Including pants, his son inherited,
For a small fee, from Hesslop's funeral home;
And my mother,
Weeping with anger, afraid of winter
For her brothers' sake:
Willy, and John, whose life and art, if any,
I never knew.

A PRAYER TO THE LORD RAMAKRISHNA

1.

The anguish of a naked body is more terrible
To bear than God.
And the rain goes on falling.

2.

When I stand up to cry out,
She laughs.
On the window sill, I lean
My bare elbows.
One blue wing, torn whole out of heaven,
Soaks in the black rain.

3.
Blind, mouth sealed, a face blazes
On my pillow of cold ashes.

4.
No!
I kneel down, naked, and ask forgiveness.
A cold drizzle blows into the room,
And my shoulders flinch to the bone.
You have nothing to do with us.
Sleep on.

IN MEMORY OF LEOPARDI

I have gone past all those times when the poets
Were beautiful as only
The rich can be. The cold bangles
Of the moon grazed one of my shoulders,
And so to this day,
And beyond, I carry
The sliver of a white city, the barb of a jewel
In my left clavicle that hunches.
Tonight I sling
A scrambling sack of oblivions and lame prayers
On my right good arm. The Ohio River
Has flown by me twice, the dark jubilating
Isaiah of mill and smoke marrow. Blind son
Of a meadow of huge horses, lover of drowned islands
Above Steubenville, blind father
Of my halt gray wing:
Now I limp on, knowing
The moon strides behind me, swinging
The scimitar of the divinity that struck down
The hunchback in agony
When he saw her, naked, carrying away his last sheep
Through the Asian rocks.

TWO POSTURES BESIDE A FIRE

1.

Tonight I watch my father's hair,
As he sits dreaming near his stove.
Knowing my feather of despair,
He sent me an owl's plume for love,
Lest I not know, so I've come home.
Tonight Ohio, where I once
Hounded and cursed my loneliness,
Shows me my father, who broke stones,
Wrestled and mastered great machines,
And rests, shadowing his lovely face.

2.

Nobly his hands fold together in his repose.
He is proud of me, believing
I have done strong things among men and become a man
Of place among men of place in the large cities.
I will not waken him.
I have come home alone, without wife or child
To delight him. Awake, solitary and welcome,
I too sit near his stove, the lines
Of an ugly age scarring my face, and my hands
Twitch nervously about.

FOR THE MARSH'S BIRTHDAY

As a father to his son, as a friend to
his friend, Be pleased to show mercy, O God.

I was alone once, waiting
For you, what you might be.
I heard your grass birds, fluting
Down a long road, to me.
Wholly for you, for you,
I was lonely, lonely.

For how was I to know
Your voice, or understand
The Irish cockatoo?
Never on sea or land
Had I heard a voice that was
Greener than grass.

Oh the voice lovelier was
Than a crow's dreaming face,
His secret face, that smiles
Alive in a dead place.
Oh I was lonely, lonely:
What were the not to me?

The not were nothing then.
Now, let the not become
Nothing, and so remain,
Till the bright grass birds come
Home to the singing tree.
Then, let them be.

Let them be living, then,
They have been dead so long.
Love, I am sick of pain
And sick with my longing,
My Irish cockatoo,
To listen to you,

Now you are all alive
And not a dream at all;
Now there are more than five
Voices I listen to
Call, call, call, call, call, call:
My Irish cockatoo.

LIFTING ILLEGAL NETS BY FLASHLIGHT

The carp are secrets
Of the creation: I do not

Know if they are lonely.
The poachers drift with an almost frightening
Care under the bridge.
Water is a luminous
Mirror of swallows' nests. The stars
Have gone down.
What does my anguish
Matter? Something
The color
Of a puma has plunged through this net, and is gone.
This is the firmest
Net I ever saw, and yet something
Is gone lonely
Into the headwaters of the Minnesota.

CONFESSION TO J. EDGAR HOOVER

Hiding in the church of an abandoned stone,
A Negro soldier
Is flipping the pages of the Articles of War,
That he can't read.

Our father,
Last evening I devoured the wing
Of a cloud.
And, in the city, I sneaked down
To pray with a sick tree.

I labor to die, father,
I ride the great stones,
I hide under stars and maples,
And yet I cannot find my own face.
In the mountains of blast furnaces,
The trees turn their backs on me.

Father, the dark moths
Crouch at the sills of the earth, waiting.

And I am afraid of my own prayers.
Father, forgive me.
I did not know what I was doing.

TO THE POETS IN NEW YORK

You strolled in the open, leisurely and alone,
Daydreaming of a beautiful human body
That had undressed quietly and slipped into the river
And become the river:
The proud body of an animal that would transform
The snaggled gears and the pulleys
Into a plant that grows under water.
You went searching gently for the father of your own agony,
The camellia of your death,
The voice that would call out to you clearly and name the fires
Of your hidden equator.

Solitary,
Patient for the last voices of the dusk to die down, and the dusk
To die down, listener waiting for courteous rivers
To rise and be known,
You kept a dark counsel.
It is not seemly a man should rend open by day
The huge roots of his blood trees.
A man ought to hide sometimes on the banks
Of the sky,
And some human beings
Have need of lingering back in the fastidious half-light
Even at dawn.

THE RIVER DOWN HOME

Under the enormous pier-shadow,
Hobie Johnson drowned in a suckhole.
I cannot even remember
His obliterated face.
Outside my window, now, Minneapolis

Drowns, dark.
It is dark.
I have no life.

What is left of all of it?
Blind hoboes sell American flags
And bad poems of patriotism
On Saturday evenings forever in the rain,
Between the cathouses and the slag heaps
And the river, down home.
Oh Jesus Christ, the Czechoslovakians
Are drunk again, clambering
Down the sand-pitted walls
Of the grave.

IN RESPONSE TO A RUMOR THAT THE OLDEST WHOREHOUSE IN WHEELING, WEST VIRGINIA, HAS BEEN CONDEMNED

I will grieve alone,
As I strolled alone, years ago, down along
The Ohio shore.
I hid in the hobo jungle weeds
Upstream from the sewer main,
Pondering, gazing.

I saw, down river,
At Twenty-third and Water Streets
By the vinegar works,
The doors open in early evening.
Swinging their purses, the women
Poured down the long street to the river
And into the river.

I do not know how it was
They could drown every evening.
What time near dawn did they climb up the other shore,
Drying their wings?

For the river at Wheeling, West Virginia,
Has only two shores:
The one in hell, the other
In Bridgeport, Ohio.

And nobody would commit suicide, only
To find beyond death
Bridgeport, Ohio.

POEMS TO A BROWN CRICKET

1.

I woke,
Just about daybreak, and fell back
In a drowse.
A clean leaf from one of the new cedars
Has blown in through the open window.
How long ago a huge shadow of wings pondering and hovering
  leaned down
To comfort my face.
I don't care who loved me.
Somebody did, so I let myself alone.
I will stand watch for you, now.
I lay here awake a long time before I looked up
And found you sunning yourself asleep
In the Secret Life of Jakob Boehme
Left open on the desk.

2.

Our friends gave us their love
And this room to sleep in.
Outside now, not a sound.
Instead of rousing us out for breakfast,
Our friends love us and grant us our loneliness.
We shall waken again
When the courteous face of the old horse David
Appears at our window,
To snuffle and cough gently.
He, too, believes we may long for

166

One more dream of slow canters across the prairie
Before we come home to our strange bodies
And rise from the dead.

3.
As for me, I have been listening,
For an hour or so, now, to the scampering ghosts
Of Sioux ponies, down the long road
Toward South Dakota.
They just brought me home, leaning forward, by both hands
     clinging
To the joists of the magnificent dappled feathers
Under their wings.

4.
As for you, I won't press you to tell me
Where you have gone.
I know. I know how you love to edge down
The long trails of canyons.
At the bottom, along willow shores, you stand, waiting for twilight,
In the silence of deep grass.
You are safe there, guarded, for you know how the dark faces
Of the cliffs forbid easy plundering
Of their beautiful pueblos:
White cities concealed delicately in their chasms
As the new eggs of the mourning dove
In her ground nest,
That only the spirit hunters
Of the snow can find.

5.
Brown cricket, you are my friend's name.
I will send back my shadow for your sake, to stand guard
On the solitude of the mourning dove's young.
Here, I will stand by you, shadowless,
At the small golden door of your body till you wake
In a book that is shining.

TO THE MUSE

It is all right. All they do
Is go in by dividing
One rib from another. I wouldn't
Lie to you. It hurts
Like nothing I know. All they do
Is burn their way in with a wire.
It forks in and out a little like the tongue
Of that frightened garter snake we caught
At Cloverfield, you and me, Jenny
So long ago.

I would lie to you
If I could.
But the only way I can get you to come up
Out of the suckhole, the south face
Of the Powhatan pit, is to tell you
What you know:

You come up after dark, you poise alone
With me on the shore.
I lead you back to this world.

Three lady doctors in Wheeling open
Their offices at night.
I don't have to call them, they are always there.
But they only have to put the knife once
Under your breast.
Then they hang their contraption.
And you bear it.

It's awkward a while. Still, it lets you
Walk about on tiptoe if you don't
Jiggle the needle.
It might stab your heart, you see.
The blade hangs in your lung and the tube
Keeps it draining.
That way they only have to stab you
Once. Oh Jenny,

I wish to God I had made this world, this scurvy
And disastrous place. I
Didn't, I can't bear it
Either, I don't blame you, sleeping down there
Face down in the unbelievable silk of spring,
Muse of black sand,
Alone.

I don't blame you, I know
The place where you lie.
I admit everything. But look at me.
How can I live without you?
Come up to me, love,
Out of the river, or I will
Come down to you.

NEW POEMS

THE IDEA OF THE GOOD

I am bone lonely
Down on the black rock.
Now once again I take
My way, my own way,
Alone till the black
Rock opens into ground
And closes and I die.
Two hundred feet below me two deer fled past just now.
I want an owl to poise on my grave
Without sound, but
In this mean time
I want bone feet borne down
Cold on stone.
I dream of my poor Judas walking along and alone
And alone and alone and alone till his wound
Woke and his bowels
Broke.
Jenny, I gave you that unhappy
Book that nobody knows but you
And me, so give me
A little life back.
Or at least send me the owl's feather
Again, and I promise I will give it
To no one. How could I?
Nobody else will follow
This poem but you,
But I don't care.
My precious secret, how
Could they know
You or me?
Patience.

BLUE TEAL'S MOTHER

How do I know it was a fox?
It might have been nothing
But the late snow.

All I know is
My friend brought home
The five blue babies, caressing their feathers.
One followed after another across
The moulting road, and they
Had no mother, they had
No father, they had only
The humpbacked old Chevrolet
They came home in.

In three days, they were gone.
A weasel got them.

The weasel turns white in the snow,
And becomes an ermine,
That some women wear dead.

Set free the weasel,
Set free the fox,
And the cold groundhog
Outwitting the sun.

Give even the living
A chance.

I, too, live,
Even in my pain.
Why, look here, one night
When I was drunk,
A bulk tree got in my way.
Never mind what I thought when dawn broke.
In the dark, the night before,
I knew perfectly well I could have knocked
The bulk tree down.
Well, cut it up, anyway.

I didn't hurt it.
I gathered it into my arms.
You may not believe this, but
It turned into a slender woman.

Stop nagging me. I know
What I just said.
It turned into a slender woman.

MOON

I am so delighted
With you, because I know you
And I know you
Came down to me, answering.
I walked up hill
After you went all the way down.
I hadn't seen you,
But I believed in you,
And I believed you were dividing three cones
Of sky down beyond
The left shoulder of the white oak
In Warnock,
Ohio, and I remember and I pray
Come down to me love and bring me
One panther of silver and one happy
Evening of snow,
And I will give you
My life, my own, and now
My beloved has come to me and we have gone walking
Below you beside the East
River in the snow, all
Three of us, leaving
Six prints of panther, kind
Woman, and happy
Man,
And I love you,
Sky full of laurels and arrows,
White shadow of cities where the scars
Of forgotten swans
Waken into feathers
And new leaves.

A POEM ABOUT BREASTS

Already she seems bone thin
When her clothes are on.
The lightest wind blows
Her dress toward the doorways.
Everybody thinks he can see
Her body longing to follow
Helpless and miserable,
Dreaming itself
Into an apparition of loneliness,
A spirit of vine wondering
At a grape here and there,
As the September spider,
The master, ascends
Her long spine.

Already she weighs more, yet
She still bows down slightly,
As I stand in her doorway.
It's not hunching, it's only
That children have been reaching
Upward for years to gather
Sweetness of her face.
They are innocent and passionate
Thieves of the secret hillsides.
Now she rises, tall, round, round,
And round again, and, again, round.

SUN TAN AT DUSK

When was the last time
You remembered you
Had gone out? A bee
Blew past me. Jays
Raised hell down stream,
You rose up
Slow out of the mountain pool.
Color of doe out of green

Against dark.
The fawn's honey weeping down stream.
I just got up. This is
When I wake.

A MAD FIGHT SONG FOR WILLIAM S. CARPENTER, 1966*

Varus, varus, gib mir meine Legionen wieder

Quick on my feet in those Novembers of my loneliness,
I tossed a short pass,
Almost the instant I got the ball, right over the head
Of Barrel Terry before he knocked me cold.

When I woke, I found myself crying out
Latin conjugations, and the new snow falling
At the edge of a green field.

Lemoyne Crone had caught the pass, while I lay
Unconscious and raging
Alone with the fire ghost of Catullus, the contemptuous
        graces tossing
Garlands and hendecasyllabics over the head
Of Cornelius Nepos the mastodon,
The huge volume.

At the edges of southeast Asia this afternoon
The quarterbacks and the lines are beginning to fall,
A spring snow,

And terrified young men
Quick on their feet
Lob one another's skulls across
Wings of strange birds that are burning
Themselves alive.

*Carpenter, a West Pointer, called for his own troops to be napalmed rather than
have them surrender. General Westmoreland called him "hero" and made him his
aide, and President Johnson awarded him a Silver Star for courage.

THE PRETTY REDHEAD

from the French of Appollinaire

I stand here in the sight of everyone a man full of sense
Knowing life and knowing of death what a living man can know
Having gone through the griefs and happinesses of love
Having known sometimes how to impose his ideas
Knowing several languages
Having travelled more than a little
Having seen war in the artillery and the infantry
Wounded in the head trepanned under chloroform
Having lost his best friends in the horror of battle

I know as much as one man alone can know
Of the ancient and the new
And without troubling myself about this war today
Between us and for us my friends
I judge this long quarrel between tradition and imagination
Between order and adventure

You whose mouth is made in the image of God's mouth
Mouth which is order itself
Judge kindly when you compare us
With those who were the very perfection of order
We who are seeking everywhere for adventure

We are not your enemies
Who want to give ourselves vast strange domains
Where mystery flowers into any hands that long for it
Where there are new fires colors never seen
A thousand fantasies difficult to make sense out of
They must be made real
All we want is to explore kindness the enormous country where
    everything is silent
And there is time which somebody can banish or welcome home
Pity for us who fight always on the frontiers
Of the illimitable and the future
Pity our mistakes pity our sins

178

Here summer is coming the violent season
And so my youth is as dead as spring
Oh Sun it is the time of reason grown passionate
And I am still waiting
To follow the forms she takes noble and gentle
So I may love her alone

She comes and draws me as a magnet draws filaments of iron
She has the lovely appearance
Of an adorable redhead
Her hair turns golden you would say
A beautiful lightning flash that goes on and on
Or the flames that spread out their feathers
In wilting tea roses

But laugh laugh at me
Men everywhere especially people from here
For there are so many things that I don't dare to tell you
So many things that you would not let me say
Have pity on me

ECHO FOR THE PROMISE OF GEORG TRAKL'S LIFE

Quiet voice,
In the midst of those blazing
Howitzers in blossom.
Their fire
Is a vacancy.

What do those stuttering machines
Have to do
With the solitude?

Guns make no sound.
Only the quiet voice
Speaks from the body of the deer
To the body of the woman.

My own body swims in a silent pool,
And I make silence.

They both hear me.
Hear me,
Father of my sound,
My poor son.

A CENTENARY ODE: INSCRIBED TO LITTLE CROW, LEADER OF THE SIOUX REBELLION IN MINNESOTA, 1862

I had nothing to do with it. I was not here.
I was not born.
In 1862, when your hotheads
Raised hell from here to South Dakota,
My own fathers scattered into West Virginia
And southern Ohio.
My family fought the Confederacy
And fought the Union.
None of them got killed.
But for all that, it was not my fathers
Who murdered you.
Not much.

I don't know
Where the fathers of Minneapolis finalized
Your flayed carcass.
Little Crow, true father
Of my dark America,
When I close my eyes I lose you among
Old lonelinesses.
My family were a lot of singing drunks and good carpenters.
We had brothers who loved one another no matter what they did.
And they did plenty.

I think they would have run like hell from your Sioux.
And when you caught them you all would have run like hell
From the Confederacy and from the Union

Into the hills and hunted for a few things,
Some bull-cat under the stones, a gar maybe,
If you were hungry, and if you were happy,
Sunfish and corn.

If only I knew where to mourn you,
I would surely mourn.

But I don't know.

I did not come here only to grieve
For my people's defeat.
The troops of the Union, who won,
Still outnumber us.
Old Paddy Beck, my great-uncle, is dead
At the old soldiers' home near Tiffen, Ohio.
He got away with every last stitch
Of his uniform, save only
The dress trousers.

Oh all around us,
The hobo jungles of America grow wild again.
The pick handles bloom like your skinned spine.
I don't even know where
My own grave is.

RED JACKET'S GRAVE

I have a deep identity
With something under
The bare stones, the
Variety of firemen,
In Buffalo, N.Y.,
Early nineteen something.

Their stones look all
Alike, the beefy faces, a few granite, sand, a little
   rich marble.

Somebody played with his callouses,
Then gouged down to find
Blacks hands. What name?
I am lonely among the black hands that are forgotten.
And lonely among the members of the Buffalo
Fire Department who
Died in World War 1.
They are not alone.

And neither is Red Jacket,
Whose noble face rises
At the entrance of the
Grave grass.

I don't know who dug
The graves of the firemen,
I don't believe Red Jacket
Would have given his left
Hand to leave his body there,
Though his name is there.

Somebody
Dug the graves.
Somebody, for maybe a dollar an hour,
Hugged the seventy-five stones,
Into the ground.

And who dug the graves?
And who wasted his black hands away among the beautiful
Roots of the elms?
And who hugged the stones
Into the ground?

TO THE AUGUST FALLEN

Below me, a pool gathers
Old wings and one leaf still shining
With a few jewels
And this light.

182

Only the feathers are heavy, and they drag
The skeleton down now, but tomorrow at dawn
Will float and rise up toward Canada.
I breathe
The waters poured out by snow hills
That are gone.

A thousand years ago,
Last night, on other huge prairies,
The Tartars of North China abandoned their rough-coated ponies
For the wind to blister, and blundered themselves off.
They groped in the snow for the shifting terraces of the moon.
They chased one another's footprints, staggering, drunk
On the fermented milk of lost mares.
They ran up the stairs of snow towers that vanished.
They huddled down between drifts,
Crying with famine.

Below me, already waterlogged,
The old leaves and the bright wing sink down between
The white hills of the south that loom now into shades,
To the fallen.

A SECRET GRATITUDE

"Eugen Boissevain died in the autumn of 1949. I had wondered already, at the
time of our visit, what would happen to Edna [Millay] if he should die first."
(Edmund Wilson)

I.
She cleaned house, and then lay down long
On the long stair.

On one of those cold white wings
That the strange fowl provide for us like one hillside
    of the sea,
That cautery of snow that blinds us,
Pitiless light,
One winter afternoon

Fair near the place where she sank down with one wing broken,
Three friends and I were caught
Stalk still in the light.

Five of the lights. Why should they care for our eyes?
Five deer stood there.
They looked back, a good minute.
They knew us, all right:
Four chemical accidents of horror pausing
Between one suicide or another
On the passing wing
Of an angel that cared no more for our biology, our pity,
    and our pain
Than we care.

Why should any mere multitude of the angels care
To lay one blind white plume down
On this outermost limit of something that is probably no more
Than an aphid,
An aphid which is one of the angels whose wings toss
    the black pears
Of tears down on the secret shores
Of the seas in the corner
Of a poet's closed eye.
Why should five deer
Gaze back at us?
They gazed back at us.
Afraid, and yet they stood there,
More alive than we four, in their terror,
In their good time.

We had a dog.
We could have got other dogs.
Two or three dogs could have taken turns running and
    dragging down
Those fleet lights, whose tails must look as mysterious
    as the
Stars in Los Angeles.
We are men.
It doesn't even satisfy us

To kill one another.
We are a smear of obscenity
On the lake whose only peace
Is a hole where the moon
Abandoned us, that poor
Girl who can't leave us alone.

If I were the moon I would shrink into a sand grain
In the corner of the poet's eye,
While there's still room.

We are men.
We are capable of anything.
We could have killed every one of those deer.
The very moon of lovers tore herself with the agony of
    a wounded tigress
Out of our side.
We can kill anything.
We can kill our own bodies.
Those deer on the hillside have no idea what in hell
We are except murderers.
They know that much, and don't think
They don't.
Man's heart is the rotten yolk of a blacksnake egg
Corroding, as it is just born, in a pile of dead
Horse dung.
I have no use for the human creature.
He subtly extracts pain awake in his own kind.
I am born one, out of an accidental hump of chemistry.
I have no use.

2.
But
We didn't set dogs on the deer,
Even though we know,
As well as you know,
We could have got away with it,
Because
Who cares?

3.
Boissevain, who was he?
Was he human? I doubt it,
From what I know
Of men.

Who was he,
Hobbling with his dry eyes
Along in the rain?

I think he must have fallen down like the plumes of new snow,
I think he must have fallen into the grass, I think he
Must surely have grown around
Her wings, gathering and being gathered,
Leaf, string, anything she could use
To build her still home of songs
Within sound of water.

4.
By God, come to that, I would have married her too,
If I'd got the chance, and she'd let me.
Think of that. Being alive with a girl
Who could turn into a laurel tree
Whenever she felt like it.
Think of that.

5.
Outside my window just now
I can hear a small waterfall rippling antiphonally down over
The stones of my poem.

SO SHE SAID

"I'd rather not. I'm confused."

I did not plow her darknesses,
Only because I'd rather not
Flop rampant on the secrecies.
They are easy enough to violate.

186

Easy enough. As when my hand
Exploded my fantastic self
I did not know nor understand
The beauty of my lonely life.

She knew me lonely so she took
My bare body into her bed,
Yet could not bear to let me look
Her over, naked. For she said
She did not know if she could bear
Two hundred pounds of the blind sky,
A man, a rock that breathes a woman's hair.
Neither did I.

And when I lay me down to die
Let me call back I might have used
The woman of a girl who loved me
Enough to let me let her lie
Alone in her own loneliness,
And mind her own good business.

I love for what I will become
In my good time when I go home
Back to my skull, that is our face.

TROUBLE

Well, look, honey, where I come from, when
a girl says she's in trouble, she's in trouble.
                              (Judy Holliday)

Leering across Pearl Street,
Crum Anderson yipped:
"Hey Pugh!
I see your sister
Been rid bareback.
She swallow a watermelon?
Fred Gordon! Fred Gordon! Fred Gordon!"

"Wayya mean? She can get fat, can't she?"

Fat? Willow and lonesome Roberta, running
Alone down Pearl Street in the rain the last time
I ever saw her, smiling a smile
Crum Anderson will never know,
Wondering at her body.

Sixteen years, and
All that time she thought she was nothing
But skin and bones.

HUMMING A TUNE FOR AN OLD LADY
IN WEST VIRGINIA

dummy-dummy-dummy-dummy-day:
gran'ma's pretty baby . . .

More than other song,
Your song, all yours.
You cast line in the water
A long time ago.
You plumbed it down, down,
Down to the fish-heads,
Stones, closed windows,
The sludge black snow.

More than other song,
Yours wakes the cat fish.
No other, not even
The splintering of ice.
Not even squeal and grind
Of chain on cold chisel
On a rust-rotten girder,
The terminal bridge.

More than other song,
Yours. I sit and listen
To the soft floppy whisper

A drowned boy made.
He rose in two pieces
A mile down the river,
One cord round his pecker
And one shoulder blade.

Now you're lost over water.
All the gouging and dragging,
Searching, finding,
Now, a mile down,
And into the other river,
I hear you still singing.
I don't die, I'm not deaf.
I scare, I go on.

Dummy-dummy comes round
Like the old blind mailman
Delivering bills that
Nobody can pay.
Black widow's the madam
Stone broke in the cat house,
And the girl with the best song
Can't sell it today,
So she gives it away.

TO A DEAD DRUNK

How carefully, fastidiously,
You lounged beside the hollow lute.
The cold aristocrats that die
Left you alone in your defeat.
Nibbling in loneliness you ground
Bitter between your outraged teeth
Early Eliot and late Pound,
Before you drank yourself to death.

Oh, plenty will remember them.
Maybe the Cyclades will not,
Nor the frail Irishmen who scream

Into our century and rot.
But someone whose triumphant name
Is Lyndon Fink Jane Adam Smith
Will pounce on your forgotten name
To write a dissertation with.

God help me too, defeated poet.
You walked with me one afternoon
Of blind stone and Ohio soot,
To visit a great lonely man.
Never you mind. Today I bought
Collected poems of Ralph Hodgson.
Now you are dead. I am not yet.
Hodgson is now. I will be soon.

Still, in Minerva, he had still
A white tree, a white miracle
Beyond a little mound of coal
(Listen, what rhymes with miracle?)
We sang all afternoon, we tossed
A willing honey under the tongue.
I must have seemed a silly ghost.
Pity me now. I was just young.

SMALL FROGS KILLED ON THE HIGHWAY

Still,
I would leap too
Into the light,
If I had the chance.
It is everything, the wet green stalk of the field
On the other side of the road.
They crouch there, too, faltering in terror
And take strange wing. Many
Of the dead never moved, but many
Of the dead are alive forever in the split second
Auto headlights more sudden
Than their drivers know.
The drivers burrow backward into dank pools

Where nothing begets
Nothing.

Across the road, tadpoles are dancing
On the quarter thumbnail
Of the moon. They can't see,
Not yet.

A WAY TO MAKE A LIVING

(from an epigram by Plato)

When I was a boy, a relative
Asked for me a job
At the Weeks Cemetery.
Think of all I could
Have raised that summer,
That money, and me
Living at home,
Fattening and getting
Ready to live my life
Out on my knees, humming,
Kneading up docks
And sumac from
Those flawless clerks-at-court, those beautiful
Grocers and judges, the polished
Dead of whom we make
So much.

I could have stayed there with them.
Cheap, too.
Imagine, never
To have turned
Wholly away from the classic
Cold, the hill, so laid
Out, measure by seemly measure clipped
And mown by old man Albright
The sexton. That would have been a hell of
A way to make a living.

Thank you, no.
I am going to take my last nourishment
Of measure from a dark blue
Ripple on swell on ripple that makes
Its own garlands.
My dead are the secret wine jars
Of Tyrian commercial travelers.
Their happiness is a lost beginning, their graves
Drift in and out of the Mediterranean.

One of these days
The immortals, clinging to a beam of sunlight
Under water, delighted by delicate crustaceans,
Will dance up thirty-foot walls of radiance,
And waken,
The sea shining on their shoulders, the fresh
Wine in their arms. Their ships have drifted away.
They are stars and snowflakes floating down
Into your hands, love.

A SUMMER MEMORY IN THE CROWDED CITY

to Garnie Braxton

She came crying down to me
Out of the dim heaven
That I had been praying
Against all afternoon.
And I cannot say
That I loved the earth much
With its hay dust
That swaled my eyes closed.
And her voice did not have
The clear sweetness
We listen to
In the books of our childhood.
Shrill, nagging, beyond pity
Or anything like it,
She lashed down, just dying

To peck my eyes out.
Oh the darling,
She would have loved to get

Her hook in me.
She coiled back into a secret
Corner of the sky
And glared down,
A mere barn swift.

Well you can't stand there.
I threw my forearms around
My face and bent forward,
Hunched into the barn
With Dave Woods
And his boy Slim Carter.
Did you see that bird, Dave?
Yes. Never mind. Look here,
Look at these pups.
They don't eat anything but milk foam.
And look how fat they keep.

Somewhere a black woman
In absolute despair
Is cursing me blind
Gnashing jaw bone on shrunk
Gums. Dave, Slim, and I
Tossed her nightmare away.
We plodded into the barn.
We clattered the dung forks
Beneath the dank joists
Where surely, somewhere,
The nest curled over the blue
Veins of somebody's
Throat and wings.

We didn't look at each other.
What the hell are we supposed to do with these birds?
They clutter the whole barn,
They spend their days flailing the pinnacles of heaven

Where the angels do nothing
But pray and sing. Faugh!
We stabbed our forks
Into the cold cow pies
And shoveled them out.

A POEM BY GARNIE BRAXTON

"Garnie, I wish I was a seagull."

"Yeah, me too.
And when you want to get warm
All you got to do
Is put on your feathers
And fly away to the south.

I been there once."

WRITTEN IN A COPY OF SWIFT'S POEMS, FOR WAYNE BURNS

I promised once if I got hold of
This book, I'd send it on to you.
These are the songs that Roethke told of,
The curious music loved by few.
I think of lanes in Laracor
Where Brinsley MacNamara wrote
His lovely elegy, before
The Yahoos got the Dean by rote.

Only, when Swift-men are all gone
Back to their chosen fields by train
And the drunk Chairman snores alone,
Swift is alive in secret, Wayne:
Singing for Stella's happiest day,
Charming a charming man, John Gay,
And greeting, now their bones are lost,
Pope's beautiful, electric ghost.

194

Here are some songs he lived in, kept
Secret from almost everyone
And laid away, while Stella slept,
Before he slept, and died, alone.
Gently, listen, the great shade passes,
Magnificent, who still can bear,
Beyond the range of horses' asses,
Nobilities, light, light and air.

ECLOGUE AT NASH'S GROVE

Cui dono lepidum novum libellum?

This is just one more
Of them, you can find them all over
America, just outside of town,
If you walk far enough.

It looks virgin, a sigh
Of maple and box-elder leaves so long held back
        and now mourning,
And the sun seeming kindly to the nibblings of rats
        at last,
As though by a change of heart.

I walked down this path, believing it.
No doubt the name belonged to some soft-eyed, sympathetic
Son of a bitch banker who stamped a Norwegian
Out of his money, this green place.

Virgin America, all right.
I wonder how much they cost, these cheap
Stones blackened in a short century.
No need to worry about standing on the dead.

The whole place is a grave, a virgin
Whose belly is black stone.
Not even the granary rats come out here any more.
Just me.

A man whom I never saw told me
The best days are the first
To flee away. I softly following
His elegy edge down the gully a little further.

He sang of war and the young prince
Far away from north Europe.
Since his day rose, I loved
The old mourner, and I wish he could mourn

For the granary rats gone home long ago.
For the Norwegians who worked this green place and
        cowered till the winter
Wind made them nervous wrecks.
For Nash, whether he was a land gouger
Or not. For my sons, who sound as unhappy as the old poet

Sometimes. For the lives who are eaten away
By the plump rats of brief years.
Whatever is left of them, it will sag into the salt cloud
When the sea comes back. And for me.

There was another with curls that clouded
His temples lonely as rich marble
And the black cement here
In Nash's Grove.

He killed his heart for the sake of living
Forever. But they do not live there, whoever
They are, and wherever forever is. This poem is a little
Darkness for them, where they do not have to weep.
Not for me, anyway.

IN MEMORY OF THE HORSE DAVID,
WHO ATE ONE OF MY POEMS

LARRY

I remember a fight
In a snow fall.
I never saw it,
But I remember.

Ed told me, angry with me
For something else.

You and some little bastard
Caught you drunk,
Nagged you outside,
And cut you up with his fists.

Down, and down, and down, in the seven
Corners of snow.

Ed explained to me
That the little son of bitches
(He has several mothers, though few)
Cut you down.

Ed knew.
If you'd lost the fight
You'd have wakened
Next morning dead.
So he didn't step in.

You rose, out of the snow.
Burly, you rose,
Knowing.

You beat him out of lament and snow blindness.

There is a little sort of
Man who drifts obscenely
Soberly into the seven corners
Of Hell, 14, Minnesota:

He selects the big good drunk man,
And cuts him down.

The giant killer is
A dirty little bastard.

I, drunk then, awake now, remember
The angel crying, as one winged sufferer to another:
Hafiz, what in hell
Are you doing in this gutter?
Where have you fallen from? With your warm voice?
And Hafiz answering the angel out of the gutter
And the north gone blind:

Watch your step, oh beloved and beyond beautiful
Bearer of the cup.
The sickle moon has torn a star from my arms.
In this wheat field, watch your step, don't whirl down
So fast. Don't walk on that ant. For she too
Loves her life. Let go, Larry.
Let go.
Let go.

THE OFFENSE

I.
All I have is the moment of my life. You
Took a moment away. Delighted, laughing,
You and I lonely by the Mississippi
        Wondered what hell was.

Hell to me was a girl whose lonely body
Needed me, somewhere, to be lonely with her.
Hell to you was the difficult, the dazzling
        Hendecasyllabic.

How in hell that we live in can we write it?
Long bones, was the phrase that I suggested.

No, you said, the bones of our lives are longer.
 What is our life, then?

We Americans, loneliness of body,
Puritans, sick at the beauty of the body,
Men and women we leave each other, lonely.
 Ray, you said lonely.

What is life? says the drunk in Sean O'Casey.
What is eternity? says Saint Augustine.
Where are you, Ray? I ask, and what the hell good does
 It do me the meter's breaking?

2.
The buds shrink under the swelling moon.
We grow smaller as the moon grows.
The young men fall down on their faces.
The rain falls down on its face,
And the girls rise.
It still looks like the lashing of winter from the ocean.
I pull my hat down. I say the hell with it, mainly because I know
That this is spring.
The wing coils all over what I can see of New Jersey,
And somebody is weeping in a darkness that I cannot see through.
I want.

3.
Listen, you didn't give
Me time enough to live
The true life that I care
To live. Even the air
That I still have to breathe
Is not my only death.
I have two. Which is which?

4.

And another thing. I still owe you that five dollars you gave me
that evening in St. Paul.

Why did you do it, Ray?

I wasn't even hungry.

TO A FRIENDLY DUN

1.

A man owes me two hundred and fifty dollars.
And I would rather be dead than ask him
To pay me back.

2.

He knows
Who he is. One afternoon in
Minneapolis, I slogged over the Tenth
Avenue bridge, I slogged upstairs
At Seven Corners, I had money enough
To climb the bitter dead
In the black snow.

3.

The snow rotted down
The black river, the love
Died in my heart as I
Slogged up the rotten
Stair. My friend said all
I got is relief meat and maybe a little more
Bean soup and
Let's go see, because
I'm hungry too.

4.

And so was I.
I drank, I ate.
I had some three hundred dollars in the bank.
At that time, all I knew

Was the rotting slit of my body.
I was dying, and my friend was hungry.
I took that fifty bucks left over
And got the hell
Out.

5.

Now three years have gone, and I have succeeded in deluding
My real body into believing it will not die.
Cold, cold, and the snow blackens into the veins
Of my city, my love, my dark city, the ocean of
Darkness, where we are all
Lonely together. My veins

Gag in my body, I love my body
As my brothers love their own
Veins gagging into the loneliness that is
Only my own life: not much, I guess,
But it is all alone, and I love it.
It may go drifting face down down the Hudson,
Dead in its own darkness, but it will go drifting dead
In its own darkness. This morning I shared
Ten dollars with a man.
Not my loneliness, which I cannot share.
Just ten bucks, which I hope he will never fear
He has to pay me back.

6.
A man who charges his brother money to save his brother's soul
Is scum.
You are scum.
I paid you.

7.
I wash my hands.

TO HARVEY, WHO TRACED THE CIRCULATION

Who is that blue
Dark, dreamer dreaming
Of me?

One afternoon I lonely found
Home when a lonely
Girl slipped her quick
Shelter down.

I love her, she is brave, she knew the moon was blooming
Under the horizon.

She said, give me my own lonely
Heart, so I can hear my heart
Beat in my left wrist.

I kissed her long
Left wrist.

Long ago the poor lonely
Brontosaurus lay down, face down, in his own
Place, death, ferns
Covered his face, secret
Body of the most delicate
Oil, the secret of steel,
The living creature who long ago smoothed
My bones into my love's lazily
Giving bones. Harvey,

There is nothing between us
But the strumming of my pulse yearning
Toward the sea. We
Are both blue.

Has any eye seen the body's eye gazing down in a daze below
The right wrist?
The blood is blue, there.

I walked once headlong into the water, longing
Or risking, if you want to risk the road,
The word road.

Just at the moment the moon
Sank into
Junk, my love rose,
I rose, and

The moon rose.

I tremble along the river.
I love breasts,
But I love most one soft
Wing of the vein.

KATY DID

1.
I was a good child,
So I am
A good man. Put that
In your pipe.

Something fell down between
Me and me,
One afternoon,
Long ago.

Uncle Shorty came home to live living in our house.
The man next door, laboring twelve hours
A day, came home.
Terrified white, he hated niggers,
And his human face, frightened with smoke,
Glared delighted in his pain through the open place
In the fence, the open place
Where I crept, sometimes,
Afraid of both.

My Uncle Shorty ran screaming back into the ruthless
House of his father, screaming
Dago! Dago!

And now my mother has told me the man next door
Walked weeping back home.

2.
Shorty the lonely is
Dead with the
Black sooted and cold mined
Man next door.

3.
I thought I was lonely, I thought I was lonely, so
I took my ghosts with me.
Whorehouse. Put
That in your pipe.
Shorty, he wanted to open a package store
Before the moon came down and the blue
Hands of the sea
Come back to gather him
And me with the black face
Of oil and grease in that place,
South Ohio, where the white man in his darkness
Scared Shorty home.

4.
I had the measles. I snuck out,
When my mother was gone, alone, and my father was gone, laboring
I found you, katydid, alone, between the two yards.
My doctor told me I looked like a tomato, and to me you looked
Into my eyes as I knelt. You were utterly silent in daylight.

5.
Annie and I have heard you sing in the dark moon
On the far side of Lake Minnewaska.
Utterly still green wings, song, moon darkly beginning,
You are she.

As for me, I have a white face
Of dark green.

MANY OF OUR WATERS: VARIATIONS ON A POEM BY A BLACK CHILD

(to my brother Jack)

(delivered as the Phi Beta Kappa poem,
College of William and Mary, December 5, 1969)

I.

from my journal, March 8, 1969: Garnie's whisper to me, while we were
watching a construction operation near Radio City. The operation had
reached that early stage at which the workmen had dug extremely deep into
the intended foundation of the building, obviously therefore to be a new
skyscraper. As Garnie watched the working men, they were far below, and,
to his eyes, as to mine, they appeared very small. About a third of them were
Negroes. And this is exactly what he whispered to me. It has to, and it can —
only it can — speak for itself:

You know,
if a blind boy
ride his bicycle
down there
he might fall into that water
I think it's water
but I don't know
they call it acid
and if that poor boy
drive his poor blind bicycle
into that acid
he drown
he die
and then
they bury him
up

2.

to the Ohio

Along Aetnaville, where I was born,
I want to spend my eternity
In hell with you.
And the moment I'm off, I'm off
Back home to my own river.

My rotted Ohio,
It was only a little while ago
That I learned the meaning of your name.
The Winnebago gave you your name, Ohio,
And Ohio means beautiful river.

In this final dawn
Of my life,
I think of two lines by the unhappy and half-forgotten
American poet, H. Phelps Putnam.

He was writing about a lonely girl's lovely place.

He cried out, "That reeking slit, wide, soft, and lecherous,
From which we bleed, and into which we drown."

Oh, my secret and lovely place, up shore from the railroad,
My bareass beach,
This is not a poem.
This is not an apology to the Muse.
This is the cold-blooded plea of a homesick vampire
To his brother and friend.
If you do not care one way or another about
The preceding lines,
Please do not go on listening
On any account of mine.
Please leave the poem.
Thank you.

Oh my back-broken beloved Ohio.
I, too, was beautiful, once,
Just like you.
We were both still a little
Young, then.
Now, all I am is a poet,
Just like you.
This morning I feel like that old child
You gathered so often
Into your rinsing arms,
And bathed, and healed.
I feel lonesome,
And sick at heart,
Frightened,
And I don't know
Why.

help.

3.

learning from MacDiarmid

The kind of poetry I want to write is
    The poetry of a grown man.
The young poets of New York come to me with
Their mangled figures of speech,
But they have little pity
For the pure clear word.

I know something about the pure clear word,
Though I am not yet a grown man.
And who is he?

The long body of his dream is the beginning of a dark
Hair under an illiterate
Girl's ear.

And everybody goes on explaining to us

The difference between a nutmeg and a squirrel,
The grown man plows down.

He longs for the long body of his dream.
He works slowly day by long day.
He gets up in the morning and curses himself
Into black silence.
He has got his guts kicked in,
And he says
Nothing. (Reader, I am a liar. He says plenty.)
He shuts up.
He dies.
He grows.

4.

This morning
My beloved rose, before I did,
And came back again.

The kind of poetry I want is my love
Who comes back with the rain. Oh I
Would love to lie down long days long, the long
Down slipping the gown from her shoulders.

But
I got to go to work.

Work be damned, the kind
Of poetry I want
Is to lie down with my love.

All she is
Is a little ripple of rain
On a small waterfall.

What do you want from me?

5.

on the way to the planetarium

That bright black boy whom I love
Came out of the grocery
On the other side of the street.

If you don't know that street,
84th and Amsterdam,
Be proud and true to yourself if you go there.
Otherwise, get through it
Fast,
Fast,
Fast as you can.
He'll catch you.
He's the gingerbread man.

That lithe white girl whom I love
Stood on the one side of 84th
And Amsterdam.

That bright black boy whom she loves
Yelled from the other side of the street:

Can Kinny come too?
Kinny's my brother

I yelled: Garnie,
The light's changing.
Get the HELL over here.

Can Kinny come too?
I ain't got nothing but my brother.

Garnie, you and Kinny get the hell over here.

I ain't got nothing but my brother.

Neither have I, get the hell over here.

And then my lithe proud love, a little darker
Than Kinny, lifted
The baby Gemela into her long and lonely arms,
And left her back home because
Outside it was raining.

6.

Gemela

Small fawn edging through the underbrush,
Small fawn secret,
My love, my love's
Secret fawn
Fell asleep on my love's white shoulder because
It was raining,
And she couldn't go with us
To raise cain on the way to the planetarium
And brood on the stars there.

Gemela face down the Hudson River
Where even the rats drift
Belly up.
Aren't they cute little pickaninny fawns
Drifting face down the Hudson with the rats
Belly up?

7.

A Message from the Mountain Pool Where the Deer Come Down

My love and I went swimming naked one afternoon
When mother and daughter came down and watched us and went away
In their own good time.
For once in our lives we did not frighten
The creation. It never occurred to them
What we might be.

I have a little time left, Jack.
I don't know what you want.
But I know what I want.
I want to live my life.

And how can I live my life
Unless you live yours?

All this time I've been slicking into my own words
The beautiful language of my friends.
I have to use my own, now.
That's why this scattering poem sounds the way it does.
You're my brother at last,
And I don't have anything
Except my brother
And many of our waters in our native country,
When they break.
And when they break,
They break in a woman's body,
They break in your man's heart,
And they break in mine:

Pity so old and alone, it is not alone, yours, or mine,
The pity of rivers and children, the pity of brothers, the pity
Of our country, which is our lives.

A MORAL POEM FREELY ACCEPTED FROM SAPPHO

(For the marriage of Frances Seltzer and Philip Mendlow)

I would like to sleep with deer.
Then she emerges.
I sleep with both.
This poem is a deer with a dream in it.
I have stepped across its rock.
The three wings coiling out of that black stone in my breast
Jut up slashing the other two
Sides of the sky.
Let the dead rise.

Let us two die
Down with the two deer.
I believe that love among us
And those two animals
Has its place in the
Brilliance of the sun that is
More gold than gold,
And in virtue.

NORTHERN PIKE

All right. Try this,
Then. Every body
I know and care for,
And every body
Else is going
To die in a loneliness
I can't imagine and a pain
I don't know. We had
To go on living. We
Untangled the net, we slit
The body of this fish
Open from the hinge of the tail
To a place beneath the chin
I wish I could sing of.
I would just as soon we let
The living go on living.
An old poet whom we believe in
Said the same thing, and so
We paused among the dark cattails and prayed
For the muskrats,
For the ripples below their tails,
For the little movements that we knew the crawdads
        were making under water,
For the right-hand wrist of my cousin who is a policeman.
We prayed for the game warden's blindness.
We prayed for the road home.
We ate the fish.

There must be something very beautiful in my body,
I am so happy.

Bleibe, bleibe bei mir,
Holder Fremdling, süsse Liebe,
Holde süsse Liebe,
Und verlasse die Seele nicht!
Ach, wie anders, wie schön
Lebt der Himmel, lebt die Erde,
Ach, wie fühl ich, wie fühl ich
Dieses Leben zum erstenmal!

Goethe